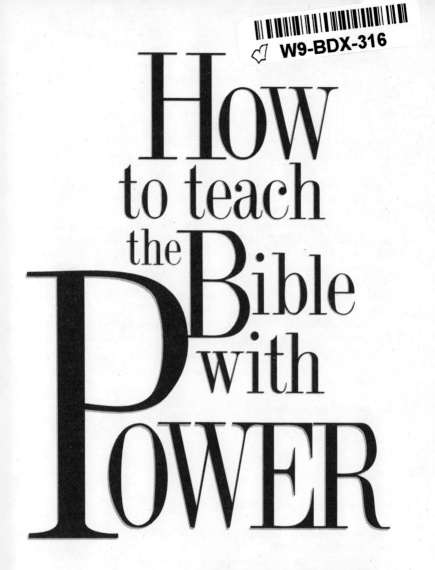

How to teach the Bible with Power

Charles H. Betz

REVIEW AND HERALD® PUBLISHING ASSOCIATION
HAGERSTOWN, MD 21740

W9-BDX-316

Texts credited to NIV are from the *Holy Bible, New International Version.* Copyright © 1973, 1978, 1984, International Bible Society. Used by permission of Zondervan Bible Publishers.

Bible texts credited to RSV are from the Revised Standard Version of the Bible, copyright © 1946, 1952, 1971, by the Division of Christian Education of the National Council of the Churches of Christ in the U.S.A. Used by permission.

Bible texts credited to TEV are from the *Good News Bible*—Old Testament: Copyright © American Bible Society 1976; New Testament: Copyright © American Bible Society 1966, 1971, 1976.

Texts credited to Weymouth are from Richard Francis Weymouth, *The New Testament in Modern Speech* (London: James Clarke & Co., 1903).

This book was
Edited by Gerald Wheeler
Designed by Patricia S. Wegh
Cover design by Willie Duke
Typeset: Cochin 12/13.5

PRINTED IN U.S.A.

99 98 97 96 95   10 9 8 7 6 5 4 3 2 1

Library of Congress Cataloging in Publication Data
Betz, Charles H., 1918-
    How to teach the Bible with power / by Charles H. Betz.
        p.   cm.
    1. Bible—Study and teaching. 2. Christian education—Teaching methods. 3. Seventh-day Adventists—Education. I. Title.
BS600.2.B44   1995
268'.86732—dc20   94-38887
                                             CIP

ISBN 0-8280-0787-X

About This Book

As you open this volume you are probably asking, "Can this book really help me?"

If you are a concerned parent, an elementary school teacher, an academy Bible teacher, a Sabbath school teacher, a pastor, or a lay-Bible instructor—this book was written to assist you in teaching the Scriptures creatively and redemptively.

I became aware of the need for such a book several years ago while searching for training materials for those who teach the Bible. And so, here it is. I sincerely hope and pray that this volume will fill a need in our homes, classrooms, churches, and Sabbath schools.

Many of our children and youth view the Bible as a rulebook. How often we preface our counsel with the words "The Bible says." (And often it is necessary.) My purpose is to help you change the current attitudes of many of our youth toward the Holy Scriptures. That's why I want to begin our discussion by talking about "The Good News Book."

Most teachers diligently study content and carefully craft their lesson plans. But few take into consideration the learner as they should. A knowledge of human development, age-level characteristics, and developmental tasks will help parents and teachers to understand and meet the felt needs of children, adolescents, and adults.

Why does peer pressure have such enormous influence on adolescents? Why are they so attracted to rock music, movies, and television? How can we enable them to resist the subtle forces of a sex-saturated society? I want to share some important information that will aid you in these areas.

Discussion and strategic questioning are crucial to creative Bible teaching. The information in this book will help you make your Bible teaching fresh, vital, and interesting.

I think you will enjoy examining the teaching techniques of Jesus. You'll be surprised to discover how often He used learning activities to help His followers discover truth. Also, I am sharing nearly 40 Bible learning activities for children, youth, and adults. Twelve of these strategies are especially designed to enable learners to clarify their values, give them practice in solving moral dilemmas, and help them establish a value system of their own. Bible-learning activities can help you transform your Bible class or home Bible study into an interesting, challenging—yes, a fun—experience.

Do your children really look forward to family worship? We are including 18 strategies to make your family devotions more creative and enjoyable.

Have you ever had the pleasure of leading a child, a teen, or an adult to Christ? Helping a child cross the threshold of conversion is one of the most thrilling things I have ever experienced. Our discussion of "The Moral and Spiritual Life of Children and Youth" will reveal some of the dynamics involved. And there is much more . . .

I am deeply grateful to my wife, Harriet, for her counsel and encouragement, and for the countless hours she spent at the word processor in producing this manuscript. And most of all, I am thankful for the guidance of the Holy Spirit—the creative and powerful Bible teacher par excellence.

> "To Children—
> "Ye are better than all the ballads
> That were ever sung or said;
> For ye are living poems,
> And all the rest are dead."
> — Longfellow

Contents

Chapter 1

The Good News Book

One rainy day I was sitting in my office feeling just a little depressed. Work was stacking up, I could sense the pressure to produce, and plans were just not working out. Life seemed as bleak as the bare trees and gloomy skies outside my window. Suddenly my door opened and my secretary walked in with a big smile. "I have good news for you," she said. In that instant the clouds seemed to vanish, and my gray mood suddenly changed to happy anticipation. And what was the good news? To be honest, I have forgotten, for it was many years ago. But the moment of joy, the big change in my mental outlook, I'll always remember.

When someone says to you, "I have good news for you," how do you respond? Good news has marvelous power to change attitudes and feelings. It is always welcome. And it's fun to be the bearer of good news. That's why I'm excited about the Bible—it is, indeed, the good news Book! Jesus and the apostles were also enthusiastic about the good news. The New Testament uses the word "gospel" (good news) more than 100 times. This book is about the Bible's good news with special emphasis on how to share it and teach it creatively.

GOOD NEWS—WE ARE NOT ALONE!

As Peter Berger said, "man finds it very difficult to

be alone in the cosmos either as an individual or in collectivities."[1] Maybe that's why even modern humanists keep bringing up the subject of God and the transcendent. Nietzsche had to admit that "a world in which God has died has become colder."[2]

Are we alone? Is there life in outer space? The idea fascinates scientists, and humanity has asked the question for millennia. And now astrophysicists have created sophisticated apparatus for receiving, analyzing, and processing radio signals from outer space. NASA has developed deep space-tracking devices—great radioscopes that scan the heavens to receive the chaotic outpouring of radio signals from the cosmos. Computers sift patiently through the data, seeking for extraterrestrial intelligence. Confronted with the fact of human existence, and that of the external universe, humanity is full of questions. We look inward and ask: "Who am I?" Glancing upward, we ponder, "Am I alone?"

Most secular humanists recognize nothing to appeal to beyond the authority of science. Human need is purely technical in nature. The notion of special divine aid "belongs to the childhood of the race." Many intellectuals claim that "man . . . arose by chance in a chance universe with only a future of chance . . ." "Nihilism accepts the conclusion that everything is meaningless and chaotic."[3] We protest such Promethean arrogance. The intellectual-humanistic climate in our society is barren and hopeless. Much contemporary art, music, and scientific literature reflects an element of despair as it speaks of "the still sad music of humanity."

Yet we have not been left alone to struggle for existence, to wrestle with life's problems, doubts, and uncertainties. As Francis Schaeffer said: "He is there and He is not silent."[4] Those who teach the Bible should lead their learners to the solid ground of faith in the Word of God and the good news about Jesus.

THE BIBLE PROVIDES A PHILOSOPHY OF HOPE

It has been said that philosophers bake no bread. But it is also true that without philosophy no bread would ever have been baked in the first place. And what is the baker's philosophy? Life is worth living! Most bakers probably do not grapple with such ultimate questions, but, like everyone else, the baker functions on a philosophical premise. Everyone operates on some kind of philosophical view. Even "Eat, drink, and be merry for tomorrow we die" is a philosophical statement and expresses the worldview of millions. (But how will such a philosophy affect behavior?)

People are as they think. Bible teachers and students should struggle with the big questions of ultimate reality. Most young people today do not stop to consider consequences—they act. They accept uncritically hand-me-down philosophies from parents, preachers, or their favorite movie stars. "It is the work of true education . . . to train the youth to be thinkers, and not mere reflectors of other men's thought."[5] Let us "grapple with great themes."[6] The Bible offers a positive worldview: a good news philosophy of hope based on the existence of the first great cause and a rational, predictable universe. God's Word contains true philosophy and true science. Some think that a system in which God directly reveals things excludes all questioning. But I would ask, "Is not Christianity a theoretical system of philosophy?" Help learners discover the data, then enable them to build a philosophy and a system of values *of their very own* based on sanctified reason and revelation. Only this will provide a solid foundation for faith.

Skillful, Spirit-directed searching of God's Word, along with honest discussion in an open nonthreatening environment, will provide an atmosphere conducive to the development of a personal philosophy. Adolescents live in a state of transition, and this is the time to help them shape a good philosophy before their ways of thinking become set and difficult to change. "Let the inquiring minds of the students be respected. Treat their inquiries with respect."[7] Group thinking—a laboratory atmosphere in the classroom—contributes to thinking/learning. One observer has said that *the Bible class, for many youth, can become an escape valve to release mounting tension before it erupts in sin and folly.*

THE BIBLE WAS DESIGNED TO MEET HUMAN NEED

Needs and satisfactions—that's the rhythm of life! Jesus said, "Your heavenly Father knows that you [have] need" (Matt. 6:32, RSV). When a mother faithfully meets her baby's needs, trust develops and bonding takes place between them. And as we recognize that our heavenly Father is meeting our needs, a similar bonding will occur.

Allan Bloom said: "There is no real education that does not respond to felt need."[8] Relating Bible truths to life's needs is a powerful motivator in any life. If students feel that Bible teaching is meeting their needs, they will give great attention to it. They will recognize that the Bible is, indeed, relevant to daily life. One of the unique aspects of Jesus as an educator was His constant concern for the felt needs of His learners. He fed the hungry, healed the sick, encouraged the depressed, and stooped to minister to the most lowly. "It was He who in the material world provided that every desire implanted should be met. . . . We need to clasp a hand that is warm, to trust in a heart full of tenderness."[9]

Lynn was a constant problem in my Bible class. Managing to fall out of his chair almost every day, he was constantly poking other children and talking out loud—he would do anything to get attention. I dreaded every class. Something had to be done! First, I made it a point to get better acquainted with Lynn's parents. As a result, I found that his home life was tragic. The family lived in a cramped little trailer. Pampered by his mother and neglected by a stern father, Lynn was the constant focus of criticism. Taking him on as a challenge, I tried to keep his mind occupied and his hands busy—helping me. Every time he did something right, I affirmed him. My strategy included eye contact, focused attention, and lots of appropriate touching. I was strict but kind. One day, as we walked down the hall after class, I put my hand on his shoulder. "Lynn, I appreciate your helping Joe with his work today. You have talent. God loves you, we love you, and I'm certain that God has a special work for you to do." In class I emphasized positive Bible role models and provided as many success experiences for Lynn as possible in order to help him feel good about himself. It was an uphill battle all the way, but I began to see some slight improvement. My experience with Lynn took place several years ago. Recently I saw him again, and we had a nice visit. Something about the way he looked at me gave me hope, as I could see that he was growing. I felt thankful for having had the privilege of sharing the good news of Jesus' love with Lynn.

GOD'S WORD PROVIDES
ENCOURAGEMENT AND ASSURANCE

Discouragement and insecurity are endemic in our

Western culture. It affects even many of our children. Recently I saw a sign on the back of a car: "Since I have given up hope I feel much better." Suicide is the second-highest cause of death among teenagers. "Discouragement is the final outcome of a process of testing and trying, of groping and hoping; it is the stage that is reached after one has hoped against hope, tried without expectation of success, and finally given up in despair. . . . The discouraged person cannot perceive the possibility of winning a battle, of ever solving his problems, of finding solutions, or even of moving toward possible solutions."[10] But thank God for the good news Book and the promise that in Christ we can find assurance and security. Let's make our Bible classes bright with assurance, the happiest class of the day or week. And the Holy Spirit will help us to present Christ as the friend of youth. Instead of young people turning to drugs, promiscuity, or alcohol, they will go to Jesus. And as we talk of Jesus, the Spirit of God will be present to bring healing in their lives.

How can we encourage our students? Note Dinkmeyer and Dreikurs' helpful suggestions: "The teacher . . . needs to understand the general philosophy underlying encouragement. Valuing, showing faith, stimulating belief in self, giving recognition for effort, utilizing the group to enhance development, pacing, and a recognition of and focus on strengths, assets, and interests are all basic principles."[11] (We will talk more about this in chapter 8.)

THE BIBLE HAS POWER TO CHANGE LIVES

As a young Christian I lived with discouragement. Finally I left the church. *I'll never make it, so I might as well have fun while I'm here,* I thought to myself for many years.

The sermons I heard and the quotations I read seemed only to make things worse. However, I stayed with the Adventist school system.

One Bible teacher was significantly different from the rest of my instructors. He presented the course "Life and Teachings of Jesus." The religion that he taught centered on a person—Jesus Christ. And the more I heard about Jesus, the better it sounded. As I listened to this man, I began to see Christianity and the Seventh-day Adventist Church in a different light. Here was hope. Instead of rules, standards, and legalism, my teacher led me to focus my attention on the Saviour. Then there was my "outside reading" assignment. I decided to use Saturday afternoons to "get my *Desire of Ages* reading out of the way," a plan I followed for several weeks. But something began to happen deep down inside. Jesus seemed to dominate the landscape. One Sabbath afternoon as I finished my reading I decided that I would try Jesus. Quietly and calmly I knelt and gave my life to Him. I told Him all about my failures but that now I was going to put my trust in Him. It wasn't anything dramatic, but I had peace and assurance for the first time. Gradually I lost interest in my secular ways. Peace took the place of anxiety, and assurance replaced my disappointments and frustrations.

God's immediate instrument was a Bible teacher who understood and loved young people, and who was able to transform doctrine into good news. The man knew how to make Jesus attractive. A big rawboned individual with a quick smile and a sense of humor, he came through as a true Christian and a friend of young people. He presented Jesus as a friend of sinners, one who was continually reaching out a helping hand. Instead of the Bible and the writings of Ellen White being a collection of impossible standards, they became a fascinating revelation of Christ. Jesus became my hero! That was good news indeed!

How Will You Be Remembered?

Who are the teachers that stand out in your memory? Take a few moments now to think back over your school days. I recall people and events associated with strong feelings much easier than factual information. As I reflect on some 20 years of academic pursuits, scores of teachers come to mind. Some were brilliant; others were dull. There were the caring and the "couldn't care less" individuals, but a few who really made a difference remain etched in my memory. One or two were scholars of national reputation, but most were ordinary mortals remembered for different reasons. I recall a professor of New Testament Epistles who could quote chapters from memory. But what stands out in my mind is the tears that ran down his cheeks as he talked about Jesus.

Then there was my ninth-grade English teacher with her smiling brown eyes. "Come on, I know you can do it! Come up and try. We'll help you." So I lumbered up to the chalkboard to diagram a sentence. A tenth-grade teacher came to visit me two or three times during one particularly difficult summer—just to be friendly. I'll always remember the warmth of his caring attitude.

And what were the qualities of the teachers who made lifelong impressions on me? Sincerity, spirituality, encouragement, caring, competence, and optimism. They were the teachers who by their lives and testimony said, "I have good news for you!" The prophet Daniel describes them well: "The wise leaders will shine with all the brightness of the sky. And those who have taught many people to do what is right will shine like the stars forever" (Dan. 12:3, TEV).

---

[1] Peter Berger, *The Heretical Imperative* (Garden City, New York: Anchor Press, 1980), p. 51.

[2] *Ibid.*, p. 51.

[3] Francis A. Schaeffer, *The God Who Is There* (Downers Grove, Ill.: Inter-Varsity Press, 1968), pp. 38, 55.

[4] ———, *He Is There and He Is Not Silent* (Wheaton, Ill.: Tyndale House Publishers, 1972).

[5] Ellen G. White, *Education*, p. 17.

[6] ———, *Evangelism*, p. 151.

[7] ———, *Fundamentals of Christian Education*, p. 390.

[8] Allan Bloom, *The Closing of the American Mind* (New York: Simon and Schuster, 1987), p. 19.

[9] White, *Education*, p. 133.

[10] Don Dinkmeyer and Rudolf Dreikurs, *Encouraging Children to Learn*, (Englewood Cliffs, N.J.: Prentice-Hall, Inc., 1963), pp. 35, 34. This valuable book was written for secular educators. It was not intended for religious education, but the principles of teaching-learning apply.

[11] *Ibid.*, p. 57.

Chapter 2

Saving Information

Walker Percy suggests that it is possible to "get all A's, and flunk life."[1] Sadly, we must admit that thousands of our children who get "A's" in Bible class are in reality failing spiritually.

Phil was one of my best friends in boarding academy. He was good-looking, a top student, and very popular—in fact, he was our student body president. But he apparently failed spiritually. He left the Adventist Church shortly after high school. To him, and to many others, Bible was just another class. As teachers *we* may be extremely aware of the significant difference. We may see our Bible classes as spiritual experiences and pray about our presentation, but from the viewpoint of a tenth grader it may be—and usually is—just another assignment. It is just facts to learn for a test. Sadly, the same principle holds true in Sabbath school and other Bible teaching situations.

I have given series after series of Bible studies to persons who never joined the church. Parents may faithfully conduct family devotions year after year only to see their children drift out of the church. "Many have eyes, but they see not; they have ears, but they hear not; they have intellect, but they discern not the hidden treasure."[2] How can we teach the Bible so that our students will discover its uniqueness, enjoy it, thrill to its message, learn to love Jesus Christ, and crown Him Lord of their lives?

A SAVING KNOWLEDGE

What do our youth need? A saving knowledge of Jesus Christ. In His prayer Jesus said, "Now this is eternal life: that they may know you, the only true God, and Jesus Christ, whom you have sent" (John 17:3, NIV). Lawrence O. Richards comments on this verse: "But the Greek word itself (*gnontes*) isn't exhausted by this meaning. It comes from a root with a broad range of uses. It is used in the Bible in the sense of coming to know information, of coming to know a person, of finding out something, of comprehending, realizing; it is even used as a euphemism of sex relations. Basic to its thought seems to be the dimension of experience: this is knowledge that involves experience."[3] In the Bible we discover truth—true information about God Himself. The nice thing is that "God does more. He presents Himself in the information. God Himself confronts us in His truth. . . . In every truth God Himself meets and speaks to us. And to every truth there is a fitting response, made to the Lord Himself."[4]

FAITH RESPONSE

Stimulus response is life's natural rhythm! It is true not only in the physical realm but also in the spiritual. Every student who hears the gospel and understands finds himself or herself confronted by God. The response will be either for or against Him. Paul tells us that even the pagans, whose knowledge of God is through natural revelation (nature and reason), are without excuse. "They exchanged the truth of God for a lie, and worshiped and served created things rather than the Creator" (Rom. 1:25, NIV). Ezekiel describes the people who listen but do not respond to God's appeals. The Lord said to the prophet: "Indeed, to them you are nothing more than one who sings love songs with a beautiful voice and plays an instrument well, for they hear your words but do not put them into practice" (Eze. 33:32, NIV).

Many of our children and youth seem unable to hear and respond. I myself sat through literally hundreds of Bible classes, and usually I left resolved to do better. But somehow I did not hear the gospel. John Wesley had the same experience for many years. He said, "I went to America, to convert the Indians; but oh! who shall convert me?"[5] Finally Wesley heard the gospel. "In the evening I went very unwillingly to a society in Altersgate Street, where someone was reading Luther's preface to the Epistle to the Romans. About a quarter before nine, while he was describing the change which God works in the heart through faith in Christ, I felt my heart strangely warmed. I felt I did trust in Christ, Christ alone, for salvation; and an assurance was given me that He had taken away my sins, even mine, and saved me from the law of sin and death."[6]

The writer of Hebrews describes the problem: "For we also have had the gospel preached to us, just as they did; but the message they heard was of no value to them, because those who heard did not combine it with faith" (Heb. 4:2, NIV).

The gospel seed may remain dormant in the heart for months or even years before it takes root. A drive through the California desert in the early spring can teach marvelous spiritual lessons. (And there is nothing more desolate than the California desert!) But when the spring rains come, a miracle happens. The desert becomes a splash of brilliant colors—a profusion of poppies, desert gold, phlox, and other desert flowers. "The desert and the parched land will be glad; the wilderness will rejoice and blossom. Like the crocus, it will burst into bloom; it will rejoice greatly and shout for joy" (Isa. 35:1, 2, NIV). Our job is to sow the seed while believing that there will come an abundant harvest.

MAKE FAITH FUN

When I was a child (I grew up in a Seventh-day Adventist home) an expression we often heard in Sabbath school and church was "warn the world." Adults told me that ours was the last warning message. I heard a great deal about the Second Advent, and people often described it in torrid terms: seven last plagues, flaming fire, hail, smoke. While it impressed me greatly, I can't say that I looked forward to it with any sense of joy. As teachers of the Word of God we must faithfully tell the truth about God's final actions in history. But how careful we must be to present a balanced gospel. Satan is ever busy giving God "bad press," and sometimes parents and teachers inadvertently aid him in the process. Our task is to remove the cloud from the face of our loving God. Remember, God's last message to a dying world will be of His character of love.[7]

Good anglers know that success takes planning and strategy. Let's give more thought to baiting the hook! Many times kids turn us off because we don't seem to understand what they're interested in. "Irrelevance" is the word I often hear. What was Jesus' strategy? He talked about people's interests: parties, food, marriage, taxes, fishing, harvesting, even front-page news—such as the man who fell among thieves on his way from Jerusalem to Jericho. What attracts children and youth today? Listen to their conversations. Pay attention to the lyrics of their songs, the books and magazines they read, their video games, sports, etc. Space travel, winter and summer sports, food, dress, beauty contests, and science fiction. Draw illustrations from these areas, and be sure you know what you are talking about.

C. S. Lewis tells the story about a schoolboy who was asked what he thought God was like. "He replied that, as far as he could make out, God was 'The sort of person who is always snooping round to see if anyone is enjoying himself and then trying to stop it.'"[8] Let's change this picture. Make saving information fun! Help students believe that "in keeping them [God's law] there is great reward" (Ps. 19:11, NIV).

TRUTH SHOULD BE APPROPRIATE

Why do we teach Old Testament narratives that deal with complex theological issues and portray God's judgments with great drama to young children? A child operating on the preconceptual level does not reason abstractly. It is my opinion that they cannot handle the complex theology involved in the story of Abraham offering Isaac. The story of the Flood depicting the death of all animals and humanity except Noah and his family, the destruction of the Egyptian army at the Red Sea, the story of Jephthah, and many of the bloody battle scenes in the history of Israel—these are strong meat. Children need the milk of the Word. Preschool children have a difficult time recognizing and understanding God's loving nature in such narratives. Early childhood should be the age of innocence. We should protect young children from the rougher aspects of the adult world.

Primaries and juniors reason concretely, so we should be extremely careful how we picture God. Earliteens are just beginning to develop the capacity for abstract reasoning. But even here we should remain cautious.

I use great care in talking about God's anger. "God's attitude to sin is described in both OT and NT in terms borrowed from the human passion of anger, indignation, and wrath. It is not to be thought of as an irrational, irresponsible action on the part of God, but rather as the manifestation . . . of that aversion to sin which is part of His character."[9] Bible information will be saving if we emphasize Jesus. Christ said, "And I, if I be lifted up from the earth, will draw *all men* unto me" (John 12:32). Jesus especially attracts young, idealistic children and youth.

KEEP THE SPOTLIGHT ON THE HERO

G. K. Chesterton said, "The love of a hero is more terrible than the hatred of a tyrant."[10] Youth will have their heroes. Bible teachers can learn a great deal from the sports page in the newspaper. Why are children so obsessed with collecting baseball cards? Hero worship, of course. And that is the way God made them. In our society most of our heroes are weaklings—though they may have bulging muscles or beautiful feminine forms. The majority are moral pygmies, and many are downright corrupt.

Recognizing our need for heroes, God has provided stories about the truly great and beautiful: Moses, Joseph, Daniel, Esther, and Mary. But even more than that, our task is to lead our youth to discover Jesus the "bright and morning star." God's principal purpose is to reveal to the human race the One "altogether lovely," "the chiefest among ten thousand." Lift up Jesus in every Bible class, and the popular gods of our culture will fall. We must help young people to see Him not merely as a superman but as the Lamb of God. He is the God-man, our great sin-bearer. "This is my Father's will, that every one who fixes his gaze on the Son of God and believes in Him should have the Life of the Ages, and I will raise him to life on the last day" (John 6:40, Weymouth). Our goal is to teach God's saving information in a life-giving way.

THE HOLY SPIRIT: OUR GREAT NEED

It is one thing to have the Spirit—every born-again Christian does—but it's quite another to enjoy the fullness of His presence. And if I read my Bible correctly, this is our birthright. Paul said to the Ephesians, "Be filled with the Spirit" (Eph. 5:18). The promise is in the command (the imperative). But to have the Spirit and to be filled with the Spirit are not the same. Egypt always has the Nile. But the Egyptians wait every year for its overflow. To have the Nile is one thing, but to enjoy its overflow is another. So with us. The Holy Spirit is surely ours, but what I long for, what my class needs, is its overflow. But before the overflow there must be an infilling.

Let me ask you a question: When you go to give a Bible study or when you stand before your Sabbath school class or walk into your Bible classroom or when you call your family for worship, are you filled with the Spirit? In writing to the church at Rome, Paul said, "I know that when I come to you, I will come in the full measure of the blessing of Christ" (Rom. 15:29, NIV). As we begin to teach Bible, do we have the full measure of the blessing of Christ? It is a serious thought, isn't it?

But to have the Spirit fully demands a price. I must be willing to crucify my sinful desires and be led by the Spirit moment by moment. Note the admonitions: "Live by the Spirit." Be "led by the Spirit." Sow "to please the Spirit."

Set our mind "on what the Spirit desires" and "keep in step with the Spirit" (Gal. 5:16, 18, NIV; 6:8, NIV; Rom. 8:5, NIV; Gal. 5:25, NIV). Here is our call and privilege. And all of this is for the here and now. So for the sake of His glory and the students in our classes, let us claim our birthright and be "filled with the Spirit." Then when we teach the Bible it will be saving information.

---

[1] (Quoted in Robert Coles, *The Moral Life of Children* (New York: Grove/Atlantic, Inc., 1986), pp. 29, 30.

[2] Ellen G. White, *Christ's Object Lessons*, p. 104.

[3] Lawrence O. Richards, *Creative Bible Teaching* (Chicago: Moody Press, 1970), p. 54.

[4] *Ibid.*, p. 56.

[5] *The Journal of John Wesley*, ed. by Percy Livingstone Parker (Chicago: Moody Press, (n.d.), p. 53.

[6] *Ibid.*, p. 64.

[7] White, *Christ's Object Lessons*, p. 415.

[8] C. S. Lewis, *Mere Christianity* (New York: Macmillan Publishing Co., Inc., 1943), p. 69.

[9] N. H. Snaith in *A Theological Word Book of the Bible,* ed. Alan Richardson (New York: Macmillan Pub. Co., 1951), p. 289.

[10] G. K. Chesterton, *Orthodoxy* (New York: Doubleday, 1908), p. 44.

The Environment for Learning

Have you ever visited a greenhouse? It's like stepping into the tropics with its warmth, high humidity, and the peculiar smell of growing things. My father was a wholesale florist. For many years I observed growing plants. I spent days transplanting petunias and other bedding plants into larger pots. We were constantly moving plants into different rooms with varied temperatures. From the experience I learned that if you want plants to prosper and bloom profusely, they must receive lots of tender, loving care.

People, like plants, require a rich environment for growth. They need an atmosphere suited to their nature and individual needs. Our responsibility as parents and teachers is to provide the optimum conditions so that each person can develop his or her unique individuality, talents, abilities, and skills. In Part Two of this book we will consider an important aspect of Bible teaching—the proper context for learning. God has entrusted children to our care for nurture. Paul expressed his desires for the believers to be "rooted and built up in him, strengthened in the faith" "to prepare God's people for works of service" (Col. 2:7, NIV; Eph. 4:12, NIV). Environment includes all the surrounding conditions and influences that affect the development of a living thing. Everything that learners experience at home, at school, or at church shapes them either positively or negatively. And, like seedlings, the first few years of human development are the most critical.

MOTIVATION

Many times I have seen my father walk through the greenhouse, pick up a potted plant, turn it over, tap it lightly, and remove the plant from the pot in order to examine the root system. Root-bound plants do not prosper. So it is with learners. The restrictive environment of a formal class setting can inhibit or destroy curiosity and spontaneity. It is so easy for Bible teaching to become perfunctory and predictable. Educators tell us that if we want to motivate students to learn, we must free them to do things that are important to *them*. By expanding the learners' options and giving them choices, we enhance their self-value and influence them to strike out on their own. Let's encourage exploration in the areas of the learners' interests and respond to the students' natural curiosity instead of always expecting them to react to our plans for them. Individuality and creativity are natural characteristics of children. They need little prodding to learn when lessons are consistent with their interests and designed for their age level and developmental needs.

When children become bored with family worship, why not allow them to plan worship around things they are concerned about? In our Bible classes we could vary the program occasionally to allow the youth to follow their own interests. "Learners are more likely to be motivated where the environment is flexible and responsive to a wide variety of backgrounds, interests, talents, development rates, readiness for learning, and response to stimuli."[1]

My mother was not a trained teacher, but she knew intuitively how small children learn. In the greenhouse we had lots of sand, and on Sabbath afternoon she would often play with us in it. She simulated the Sea of Galilee by placing a piece of glass in the sand. Then she invited us to plant "trees" around the lake. Mother used stick people to represent Jesus and the disciples and a little piece of wood to depict the boat. Each of us would take turns moving the "boat" across the lake. Afterward she would tell us the wonderful story of Jesus calming the storm. She talked to us about trusting Jesus and assured us that we would never face a problem in life that Jesus couldn't take care of. Why do these things stand out in my memory? It is because Mother knew how to create an atmosphere for learning. I call it "fun." We learned through touch and feel and from a kind, caring parent. The best learning environment is not a classroom. As often as possible take children outdoors. Examine trees, flowers, insects, cobwebs, and water sparkling in the sunlight on the grass.

Plan for your seventh- or eighth-grade girls to research the apparel women wore in Bible times. Let them learn about their jewelry, flowers, musical instruments, and foods. Encourage the boys to discover what the Bible tells about animals, sports, business transactions, birds, and plants. Bible professions, agriculture, building, herbs, nutrition, and trades will also fascinate them.

What do these things have to do with an environment for learning? Quite a bit. An environment must challenge, excite, and encourage curiosity. Create opportunities, as far as possible, for children to wonder, to explore, to raise questions, and to make discoveries.

Allow them to follow their own interests. Our job is to entice learning, to provoke independent research.

The Bible is indeed a fascinating book. As teachers our challenge is to provide an environment rich with resources that will reward curiosity and stimulate children to independent study. Provide the resources for independent research: *National Geographic*; *The New Manners and Customs of Bible Times*, by Fred Wight and Ralph Gower (Moody Press); *The Encyclopedia of Bible Life*, by Madeleine S. Miller and J. Lain Miller (Harper). Also have available a good encyclopedia, *Jesus and His Times* (a Reader's Digest publication), a good Bible dictionary, etc.

A CHALLENGE OR A THREAT

Every child needs a challenge. I learn a great deal about children by watching them at play. (Play is the "work" of children.) Let's take a hint from their natural bent and provide a challenging atmosphere for Bible learning. Challenges, of course, must be realistic and appropriate for the age and sex. A challenge beyond the child's ability will become a threat. What is a stimulating challenge for one child may threaten or bore another. (This is one of the reasons for providing options.) One thing is certain: Bible study must never be a threat to anyone. I know we need to make sure that children learn a certain amount of factual information and that there should be some kind of accountability. But as far as possible, let's remove the threatening atmosphere. If children feel anxious or worried about grades—and they are doing their best— they may not hear God speaking to them. On the other hand, Bible class cannot be all fun and games. The "carrot and stick approach" is probably the best. We repeat: "Make Bible learning fun."

ACCEPTANCE

When a child—especially an adolescent—comes into a learning situation, his or her big question is: "Will I be accepted?" One educator said that the way people treat us is as much a part of the environment as the learning materials or the space provided.

Many children live with indifference or outright rejection. When they enter any kind of Bible class, they wonder, "Will this be any different? If they really knew me, they would reject me." Learners will never feel that *God* accepts them unless they know that *we* do also.

A child's perception of the teacher's feelings toward him or her has a powerful effect on academic performance. If the youngster concludes that the teacher has little confidence in his or her ability and does not believe that he or she can do well, the child will hesitate to even try. A recent study "revealed a positive and significant correlation between children's perception of teachers' feelings toward them and self-perception. It was also concluded that the more favorable the child perceived teacher feelings toward him, the better his academic achievement and classroom behavior."[2]

LEARNING AT HOME

Three-year-old Timmy loved to have his daddy tell a story at bedtime. One particular story he enjoyed greatly, and every night he would ask for the same story. After several nights the father became weary of repeating the story, so he turned on a tape recorder—unbeknown to the child. The next night when Timmy asked for the same story again, he placed the tape recorder on the floor and started it. Timmy listened intently for two or three minutes and then began tugging at his daddy's newspaper. "What's wrong, Timmy? Can't you listen to

Daddy's voice on the tape recorder?"

"But Daddy, the tape recorder doesn't have a lap." A father's lap is the best environment for learning.

When a family loves and values the child, the child feels himself or herself to be a valuable person, thus building confidence and self-respect. Being loved by father, mother, grandparents, uncles, aunts, brothers, and sisters helps a youngster to become a loving person. An African proverb says that it takes a whole village to raise a child.

Children need a stimulating, creative environment because curiosity is the foundation for learning. Many a budding scientist has gotten started at home, where parents encouraged him or her to get acquainted with insects, flowers, birds, and stones. "Let's look it up." "Let's examine it more closely." Such responses create a desire for learning that will stay with a child for life. A magnifying glass will help a child to discover God's wonders in tiny things. And a pair of binoculars or an inexpensive telescope with which children can examine the craters on the moon or the rings of Saturn produce lasting challenges.

Books, magazines—especially *National Geographic*—helped me to get acquainted with the world in which I lived. Dictionaries, maps, a globe—all of these set up an ambience for intellectual growth. Of course, we had Bibles, Sabbath school papers, and the Sabbath school lesson quarterlies available. We listened to classical music, and often we went to concerts.

It has been said that a talking family is a "thinking family." Lots of discussion of interesting topics at mealtime offers a wonderful environment for learning. (Television blaring away during mealtime prevents family closeness and communication.) A sense of humor and a good "belly laugh" will relieve tension and bring families closer together.

Many things produce an atmosphere for learning: adequate resources, lots of choices, challenges, acceptance, smiles, listening, fairness, and most of all, loving and caring people. We are all in God's "greenhouse." God is the great caretaker. Let's do our best as parents and teachers to help provide an atmosphere for luxuriant spiritual, intellectual, and cultural growth.

---

[1] Calhoun C. Collier, *Teaching in the Modern Elementary School* (New York: MacMillan, 1969), pp. 217, 224.

[2] *Ibid.*, p. 224.

Chapter 4

The Power of Caring

L eo Tolstoy, in one of his stories, writes of wealthy Russian ladies who cry at the theater but are oblivious to their own coachmen sitting outside in the freezing cold. He contrasts sentimentality with genuine caring. As Rollo May says: "Sentimentality is thinking about sentiment rather than genuinely experiencing the object of it."[1]

It is easy for Christians to luxuriate in religious sentiment. Shedding a tear during a sermon, we discuss the needs of others from inside our spiritual cocoons. We feel but we seldom act. While it is easy to talk, it is so hard to get moving. But a deep sense of caring will prompt us to action like hunger moves us to a table. Your 10-year-old boy looks at you with pleading eyes: "Daddy, would you play with me?" You think of all you have to do, but true caring causes you to get down on the floor and bring joy to a 10-year-old heart. Caring overcomes inertia. The question is Does someone or some thing really matter to me?

And what is caring? Morton T. Kelsey says, "The love that we are talking about refers to that complex of emotions, attitudes, movements of will and actions in which we reach out to others in a caring, concerned manner, desiring to let other people know that we care about them and wish to facilitate the achievement of their potential."[2] Carl Rogers calls it "prizing—'unconditional positive regard'"[3] Our great danger as Christians is in following the lead of an impersonal society. How many times lately have you heard the expression "I couldn't care less"? Rollo May says: "When we do not care, we lose our being; and caring is the way back to being . . . [and] will and wish cannot be the basis of caring . . ."[4] Caring is the focus of love. It is "love in work clothes." Love is something you do. It is giving consolation without expecting anything in return.

According to the Valuegenesis study, the "climate" of the home, the church, and the school greatly influences a child's level of faith maturity. One of the saddest facts coming from the Valuegenesis study is the feeling that prevails among our children and youth that our churches and schools lack a caring atmosphere. Only 23 percent of our youth in grades 9-12 perceive that teachers in church are really caring and supportive. The figures are somewhat better in our schools and homes: 57 percent and 61 percent, respectively.[5]

CARING ENHANCES LEARNING

A group of students from Pacific Union College organized a program called "Project Outreach." One of their projects was to work with disadvantaged children in Oakland's inner city. They went from door to door inviting the children who wanted help with their reading, math skills, spelling, etc., to come to a nearby public school for special help.

A group of 25 or 30 children showed up with their parents. Students from the education department of the college began remedial instruction. One of our student instructors began to work with a little 8-year-old Black girl to help her memorize the multiplication table through the aid of flash cards. The young college woman used every strategy she could think of, but the little girl with pigtails and sad brown eyes just couldn't seem to learn. The student instructor finally put down the flash cards, picked the little girl up in her arms, and asked her if she'd like a story. Her face brightening, the child said, "Oh, please tell me a story!" So she told of her life on the farm with the cows, horses, and the chickens, and other interesting events of her childhood. Later she said, "I could feel her little body relaxing as she snuggled up close to me." After about a half hour of holding her close and telling stories, the college student suggested they try the multiplication tables. "The results were dramatic," the PUC student later reported. "Her retention factor increased measurably."

"Recent research has pointed out some interesting facts about learning. A child who is insecure, fearful, and hostile usually has great difficulty in learning, no matter how capable the teacher or adequate his methods. It has been demonstrated that when the teacher *first* works on the relationship and the child feels that 'here is one person who really cares about me, here is one person I can really trust,' his mind seems to unlock and he begins to learn."[6]

Note the words of Ellen White: "You must win their affection, if you would impress religious truth upon their heart."[7] Carl Rogers says that teachers must create the conditions for learning. He emphasizes that experience and feelings are the most important ingredient in learning. Rogers' belief is that "traditional learning is so impersonal, cold, and aloof that it really goes in one ear and out the other." According to him, we learn only what is really important and relevant to us as people. Thus he reminds us that "we can't go through the motions and pretend we like children or listen to their feelings and emotions halfheartedly; we have to really mean it for the process to work."[8]

HOW TO CARE

One of the first steps in learning how to care is to accept people as they are. It was hard for me to accept rowdy, divisive, and hyperactive Lynn. But the best favor that I could give him was to do exactly that—accept him as he was and assume that he was going to improve. And I found that if I operated on this assumption, it helped to correct the problem. Of course, this means some bumps and bruises on the part of the teacher. But no one can know the love of God until he or she has experienced the love and acceptance of another human being. Yes, it is work to really care.

Dr. Ross Campbell, a child psychiatrist, declares that unconditional love is the foundation of personal growth. He tells a story about Tom and his grieving parents. They said that he was a good boy, content, and never gave them any trouble until he got to junior high. Then he began to disobey, talk back, lie, steal, and drink alcohol. "He is so sullen and quiet," the grieving parents explained. "We've tried everything: . . . First we spanked him. Then we took away privileges like television. . . . What did we do wrong? Are we bad parents? God knows we've tried hard enough."[9]

After the parents left, Dr. Campbell talked with Tom. Finally it came tumbling out: "No one really cares about me except my friends."[10]

Depressed, Tom had longed for a close, warm relationship with his parents. "So none suspected that Tom did not feel completely loved and accepted. Despite his having parents who deeply loved and cared for him,

Tom did not *feel* genuinely loved."[11] They gave him everything he needed except unconditional love. When he did right, they affirmed him, but when he made mistakes, they shamed him. Why? Because they loved him and wanted him to improve, of course.

Daily each child questions his or her parents and teachers: "Do you love me?" The child asks by his or her behavior, and we usually respond by our own behavior. Dr. Campbell gives a helpful illustration when he suggests that everyone has an "emotional tank." The tank, of course, is only a metaphor, but it refers to emotional needs. And when these needs get met through love, understanding, and discipline, the child feels accepted and the emotional tank remains full. Campbell gives us three clues on how to keep the tank full: eye contact, physical contact, and focused attention.[12]

EYE CONTACT

Have you noticed how newborn children stare at everything? Their little eyes will follow you all around the room. What are they looking for? You guessed it — another pair of eyes into which they can gaze. Eye contact is the primary source of emotional development for the tiny baby. The more eye contact the parent makes with the child, the more secure the child becomes. And what do we mean by eye contact? Well, it is simply looking into the eyes of another human being. When we use eye contact to communicate love and warmth, it nurtures the other person, be it spouse, friend, or child. Unfortunately, many parents use eye contact to punish: "Look at me. Now go and do as I say." We use eye contact when we give instructions or when we reprimand or criticize, but rarely do we give solid eye contact to convey tenderness, caring, and unconditional love.[13]

PHYSICAL CONTACT

You have probably seen the bumper sticker asking, "Have you hugged your kid today?" The question points up a vital need for children, youth, and even adults. God gave us hunger pangs to lead us to the kitchen. He also placed within each of us the need to be touched—skin hunger. Numerous tests demonstrate the absolute necessity for babies to be touched and held. Child psychiatrists have found that the majority of children suffer from touch deprivation. Many parents touch their children only when necessary—helping them to dress, undress, or get into a car. But touching is one of the best ways to show the unconditional love that the child so desperately needs.

Some people are touchers by nature. Others withdraw. But Jesus was a toucher. He laid His hands on the heads of the disciples when He ordained them. He touched the lepers and the blind, and washed the disciples' feet. Let us take every opportunity to make physical contact with our children—appropriate contact, of course. We are not talking so much about hugging and kissing—rather a simple touch on the shoulder, a gentle poke in the ribs, or a tousle of the hair. Small boys especially require lots of touching. Research points up the fact that little girls receive much more physical affection than boys, one reason that young boys (3 years to adolescence) have many more problems than girls. "Five to six times as many boys as girls are seen in psychiatric clinics around the country." Boys need "'boy-style' physical contact such as playful wrestling, jostling, backslapping, and playful hitting, and boxing, or bear hugs."[14]

FOCUSED ATTENTION

Our most precious commodity is time. And it takes

time, and lots of it, to give children and youth the focused attention they need. And what do we mean by focused attention? It means offering a child our undivided
attention so that he or she feels that we really care.
Children or youth need to know that they are important
in their own right and worthy of attention. Focused attention is not something that's easy or natural—it takes
time and effort. It is much easier to offer gifts than to
give our full focused attention to a battling 2- or 3-year-
old, a hyperactive 6-year-old, or a sulking adolescent.
Campbell tells about a boy who jumped in his daddy's
lap and started kissing him repeatedly on the cheek.
After a few moments the father became exasperated,
pushed him away, and said, "What are you doing?"

"Oh, Daddy, don't you know? It's your birthday and
I'm giving you 50 kisses!" But the father was tired and
frustrated with the day's work, so he pushed the child
away. A few moments later the 8-year-old got on a bicycle, rode out into the street, and died in a tragic accident.
You can imagine the terrible grief of that father.[15]

A child spells love t-i-m-e. Plan your time. Give your
children the focused attention they need. This is especially
vital with the nondemanding and passive middle child.

LISTENING

It has been said that "listening is participating in another person's life." Active listening is difficult and demanding. Why do parents, teachers, and preachers find
it so difficult to truly listen? Perhaps it is because we are
supposed to be authority figures. One reason it is hard
for me to listen carefully is that I run the risk of having
to change my mind. The teacher or parent unwilling to
change, who has his or her mind made up, will find it
very difficult or even impossible to listen.

Have you ever felt that a teacher was not really listening to what you had to say—that the adult was really just waiting for you to stop so he or she could go on "telling you"? This is monitoring conversation—not listening. Some parents and teachers just listen enough to refute what is being said. Others pay attention "selectively." They make no genuine effort to learn what the speaker thinks.

Listening helps me to (1) discover where the learner is—his or her thoughts and feelings, (2) learn from the student, (3) demonstrate that I am not trying to manipulate people, and (4) indicate to my class that I really want to understand their viewpoint.

An appropriate response in listening would be an occasional request for clarification—to get the facts and to help the learner explore them. "Can you clarify this? Is this what you mean?" Restatement is another way to truly understand. "Do I understand you to say that . . .?" A neutral stance will encourage the listener. "I see." "I understand." "That's interesting." Reflective listening tells the speaker that you grasp the feelings behind the words. "You feel that . . ." "It was shocking, wasn't it?"

The worst offense the listener can commit is to interrupt, give advice, etc. "If I were you, I would . . ." A good listener will never pass judgment or offer advice unless asked. And don't jump to conclusions. Listening is an art, a skill, and it can be learned. But it takes practice, self-control, and much prayer. When it is all over, the bottom line is "Did the other person really feel listened to?"

"Listening is a magnetic and strange thing, a creative force. . . . When we are listened to, it creates, makes us unfold and expand. Ideas actually begin to grow within us and come to life. . . . It makes people happy and free when they are listened to. . . . There are brilliant people who cannot listen much. . . . These brilliant performers, by not giving us a chance to talk, do not let us express our thoughts and expand; and it is this expressing and expanding that makes the little creative fountain inside us begin to spring and cast up new thoughts and unexpected laughter and wisdom." [16]

CARING AT SCHOOL, SABBATH SCHOOL, AND AT HOME

A few teachers especially stand out in my memory. One of them was my academy typing teacher, Carolyn Hopkins, at La Sierra Academy. I was a tall, gangly teenager, socially inhibited and extremely self-conscious. Since I was not well coordinated, typing was not my favorite subject, and I was not doing too well. But Miss Hopkins, as we called her, always had a word of encouragement for me. I still remember her standing beside me with her hand on my shoulder, saying, "You're doing all right. Just keep at it. You have many other skills to develop." She had a wry sense of humor and hardly ever smiled, but her sparkling brown eyes conveyed love and caring. Famous for her cooking, she loved to entertain students on Saturday night. Finally I was included in a group invited to her home. The food was fabulous, the games were fun, and I had a good time. (Sometimes the way to a student's heart may be through his stomach.)

Teachers of the good news will recognize and focus on the strengths of their learners rather than their weaknesses. Note the words of Don Dinkmeyer and Rudolf Dreikurs: "Teachers are inclined to feel it is their duty to point out mistakes. They frequently consider diagnosing errors as the major concern. If the relationship with a child is primarily one of pointing out mistakes, the relationship will obviously not be a pleasant one. Adequate learning requires concentration on what is correct along with the awareness of errors. It is suggested that much can be gained from consciously seeking each individual's assets."[17]

Most people want to be loving and truly caring, but they don't know how. Our hearts cannot originate nor produce true love because it is only of heavenly origin. "Love is a precious gift, which we receive from Jesus."[18] I pray that I may not run away from the bumps and bruises that may come from caring. It is my privilege to become the "wounded healer." Russell H. Argent quotes Os Guinness as saying: "No other God has wounds."[19] "Dear friends, let us love one another, for love comes from God. Everyone who loves has been born of God and knows God. Whoever does not love does not know God, because God is love" (1 John 4:7, 8, NIV).

[1] Rollo May, *Love and Will* (New York: Doubleday, 1989), p. 288.

[2] Morton T. Kelsey, *Caring* (New York: Paulist Press, 1981), p. 15.

[3] Carl Rogers, *A Way of Being* (Boston: Houghton Mifflin Co., 1980), p. 116.

[4] May, pp. 288, 286, 287.

[5] *Valuegenesis: Report 1*, pp. 28-30.

[6] Charles H. Betz, *Teaching Techniques for the Adult Sabbath School* (Hagerstown, Md.: Review and Herald Pub. Assn., 1988), p. 35.

[7] White, *Fundamentals of Christian Education*, p. 68.

[8] Carl Rogers, in Richard C. Sprinthall and Norman A. Sprinthall, *Educational Psychology: A Developmental Approach* (Reading, Mass.: Addison-Wesley Pub. Co., 1974), pp. 256, 257.

[9] Ross Campbell, *How to Really Love Your Child* (Wheaton, Ill.: Scripture Press, Inc., 1978), pp. 9, 10.

[10] *Ibid.*, pp. 10, 11.

[11] *Ibid.*, p. 12.

[12] See Campbell, pp. 32, 37-65.

[13] See Campbell, pp. 37, 38.

[14] Campbell, p. 47.

[15] See Campbell, pp. 55-59.

[16] Brenda Ueland (appeared in a Manila, Philippines, newspaper, 1983).

[17] Dinkmeyer and Dreikurs, *Encouraging Children to Learn*, p. 55.

[18] Ellen G. White, *The Ministry of Healing*, p. 358.

[19] Russell H. Argent, *Journal of Adventist Education*, April/May 1983, p. 47.

Chapter 5

The Nature and Needs of Children

There is some mysterious sense in which the creation is reechoed in the birth of every child," says Donald M. Joy.[1] As we watch children at play, hear their happy voices, observe their innocent spontaneity, we can learn something about God and the wonder of His plan for us. "Unless you change and become like little children, you will never enter the kingdom of heaven" (Matt. 18:3, NIV). Childhood learning is of supreme importance. In this chapter we want to talk about children—their nature and needs, what they can learn, and when and how they do so.

The idea of God fascinates children. And they are most susceptible to the influence of the Holy Spirit in their early years. You need not convince a little child that God exists. Children accept the teachings of the Bible and the value of prayer without question. Mounting evidence suggests that even very young children are capable of religious experience. "You are to teach your little ones to know Christ. This work you must do before Satan sows his seeds in their hearts."[2] Donald Joy says that "children are especially capable of such experiences because of the very nature of the development of the human mind. . . . [Young] children have difficulty distinguishing between reality and fantasy. They are creative and imaginative and indulge in magical explanations, inventing a wide range of supernatural persons and events. This capacity makes them highly susceptible to belief both in Santa Claus and in God. . . . It will be important that [the child's] religious environment be stable during these years and that he have wide exposure to authentic adult faith. Where these conditions exist, he will separate fantasy from faith naturally and easily as his mind grows."[3]

David Heller tells us that "the spiritual awareness that can develop in your child is infinite — it can grow as deep as his or her imagination."[4]

Here are 16 typical types of questions that children ask about God: 1. Does God have a nose? Does He have gray hair, or is He bald like Grandpa? 2. Does God get mad very easily? 3. Does God really hear me when I pray, or is He busy listening to other people? 4. Why does He say no so often? 5. Did God write the Bible, or did He have some helpers? 6. Why did God create the devil? 7. Does God have anything to do with war? 8. Is God like Jesus? 9. Is anything too hard for God? 10. Does God have a mother? 11. Does God still love kids when they are bad? 12. Is heaven very far away? Can spaceships go there? Does God stay in heaven, or does He travel around? 13. Can God wake up dead people? 14. Do you think God ever cries? 15. Is God real strong? 16. Will prayer help God to know me better?

Such questions are important to the child. They deserve a serious, thoughtful answer. Remember, when a child asks a question, he or she is ready to learn. So listen carefully and respond with love and caring.

ADAPT TO THE CHILD

A 4-year-old boy was watching an educational program on television with his parents. It showed a surgeon carefully lifting out the patient's heart. The little child, with serious brown eyes, said, "Daddy, is he giving his heart to Jesus?"

Another boy asked his mother in church, "Is this really God's house?"

"Why, yes, Peter. Why do you ask?"

"Well, when I come, I never find Him at home."

A Bible school teacher told the story of the fall of Adam and Eve and their expulsion from the Garden of Eden, then asked the children to draw a picture representing the story. A 5-year-old produced a picture of a car with a man sitting in the driver's seat and a man and woman in the back seat. The teacher asked Sally to tell about her picture. "Well, it is just like you said in your story, God drove Adam and Eve out of the garden."[5]

The preconceptual child takes things extremely literally. Often we think children understand what we have taught them, but we later may find that they learned something quite different. The apostle Paul said, "When I was a child . . . I reasoned like a child" (1 Cor. 13:11, NIV). "In His teaching He [Jesus] came down to their level. He, the Majesty of heaven, did not disdain to answer their questions, and simplify His important lessons to meet their childish understanding." "Song and prayer and lessons from the Scriptures were to be adapted to the opening mind."[6]

God has a timetable for learning based on the stages of development. Parents and teachers should bear in mind that the preoperational child (3 to 6 years of age) is unable to form concepts. Preschool children pick up bits of information about God, Jesus, heaven, the church, etc., but they are unable to organize it into a meaningful unified whole. They tend to be syncretistic, linking events or experiences that do not belong together. Time, distance, and numbers have little meaning to the preconceptual child.

It is obvious, then, that we must not expect too much of children 3 to 7 years of age. We should remember that their thinking is fragmentary and discrete. The child this age wants to understand who God is, but is not yet able to piece all the information together. This age is an excellent time to create an awareness of God and to provide accurate data concerning Bible events.

WHAT CAN CHILDREN LEARN ABOUT GOD?

The toddler learns about God primarily through the warmth and love of parents, Sabbath school teachers, and other adults. Basic trust is the first "theological concept" that a human being grasps. It comes in the mother's arms—through her loving care and attention. As the little one grows older, he or she discovers the wonders of God's world. There are so many things to see, touch, and smell.

Billy, who is 3, can know that God made him, that God made everything in the world, and that God loves him. Stories, pictures, and conversation help him to sense God's love through his receiving food and care from parents and adults. He can understand that prayer is talking to God. His mother uses simple, short phrases of thanksgiving, like "Thank You, God, for our juice." Billy can comprehend that Jesus is his special friend even though he cannot see Him. The child can know that the Bible is a special book that tells him about God and Jesus. He can understand that church is a special place where he learns about God and Jesus and the

Bible. By experiencing kindness from others, Billy is learning to be kind himself.

Four-year-old Karen can know that God made her and loves her. She can recognize that when she is praying she is talking to God. At this time she can begin to formulate her own simple prayers. Her mother helps her in phrasing them. She tells Karen that God hears her prayer and that Jesus is her special friend. Karen can learn that God wants her to do things for Him and obey His rules. The child can grasp the fact that the Bible is a book that contains God's message. She can learn that the church is God's house, and that God wants her to be quiet while she worships Him in church. Her mind is capable of realizing that God gave parents to care for her and pray for her. In addition, she can comprehend that God wants her to obey her parents, and that she sins when she disobeys Mother or Father. She can learn that she is to be forgiving, kind, and sharing, and that she can pray for others. Even at her age she can understand the concept that some angels are good and others are bad. And that Satan (the devil) is a bad angel who did not want to please God.

THE PRECONCEPTUAL PERIOD

Jean Piaget identifies the period from 2 to 7 as the intuitive or preoperational period, the 7 to 11 as concrete operational, and the 11 to 16 as the period of formal operations. As a child learns to talk, he or she gains a valuable tool for understanding the world. Language provides the ability to explore ideas. "One study of 6,000 children between the ages of 3 and 12 revealed that 4- and 5-year-olds asked more questions about God than any other age group."[7] But teachers must remember that children of this age level have little concept of

time, distance, numbers, and reversibility. To say that
Jesus lived 2,000 years ago is pointless. A child may tell
you that he or she is 5 years old but still have little concept of time. The youngster is probably only repeating
what someone else has said, and will probably have little grasp of even as short a period as 30 minutes.
Children at this age still cannot think conceptually.
Their reasoning rests on intuition and immediate and
unanalyzed impressions. For example, when Peggy, age
5, encountered two glasses of the same size filled to the
same level with water, she correctly observed that each
contained the same amount of water. But after she had
observed one of the glasses being emptied into a taller or
slender glass, she said that the taller or slender glass
contained more water than the other. Her prelogical
reasoning of the perceived data is an incomplete intellectual construction.

By the time Peggy is 7 or 8 years of age she will
begin to think in literal, or concrete, terms. It is an important transition in her life as she moves from preconceptual to the concrete, from perception to intellectual
operations. Now conceptualization is possible, however
limited. She has limited verbal reasoning, however, and
is still poor at generalizing beyond particular situations
or examples. Her thinking processes are restricted to
physical action that she can internalize.

Children of 8 or 9 can learn that 1. "God is all-pow-
erful, all-wise, and everywhere. 2. God is present with
them at all times. 3. God wants them to pray each day.
4. God the Holy Spirit is a person who is a spirit. 5.
Jesus died on the cross for sin. 6. Jesus loves them even
when they sin. 7. The Bible is God's Word and the Bible
is a true book. 8. Parents are to the child what God is to
the parents. 9. Church is like a school, except that they

learn about God and the Bible. 10. Others include a wider world far beyond the community. 11. Good angels protect God's people. 12. Heaven is for those who have accepted Christ as their personal Saviour."[8]

THE VALUE OF READING ALOUD TO CHILDREN

A Chicago school superintendent once said, "If we could get our parents to read to their preschool children 15 minutes a day, we could revolutionize the schools."

But why read aloud? Listen to these dismal statistics. The United States is the wealthiest of countries, with more automobiles, television sets, and electronic gadgets than any other nation in the world. Yet two out of every three children can't read, won't read, or hate to read. One out of every five American adults is functionally illiterate. That means that 20 percent of our adults cannot even read the directions on a can of soup. Furthermore, another 34 percent are only marginally literate—barely able to address an envelope.[9]

Why is it that we spend millions of dollars in teaching children how to read but so few choose to read? Obviously something is wrong. It appears to me that we have concentrated on teaching children how to read but have failed to help them *want* to read. Katherlyn Randalph is a fifth-grade teacher in the Boston public schools. Her students scored nearly twice as high as other Boston reading classes and better than 88 percent of the nation's fifth grades. "I always find the time to read for 10 or 15 minutes a day," she explains. "Excitement is a very contagious thing in a classroom, and children are immediately infected by it. My enthusiasm shows children that classwork is not just doing something with kids *they should like*—teachers like it too."[10] If reading aloud to children stimulates their interest, their emotional development, and their imagination, why is it that parents and teachers don't do more of it?

TALK WITH YOUR CHILDREN

Who talks to your children? The television, cassette player, the video, your computer, wind-up toys—they all talk *to* the child. Yes, their schoolteachers and Sabbath school teachers are all center stage in communicating to your children. Group discussion, as valuable as it is, however, doesn't fill the bill. Harvey S. Wiener, in his valuable book *Talk With Your Child*, says, "Talking and learning depend on each other. Are you satisfied that you're talking enough with your child now? In general, family statistics in this regard are pretty grim. American mothers, says the Department of Education, spend less than 30 minutes a day talking with their children. Fathers spend even less than that—about 15 minutes a day."[11] And why is it important to talk with your children? First of all, Scripture admonishes us: "These commandments that I give you today are to be upon your hearts. Impress them on your children. Talk about them when you sit at home and when you walk along the road, when you lie down and when you get up" (Deut. 6:6, 7, NIV).

Specialists in child development are unanimous in their emphasis on the vital importance of talking with children. Conversation shares the fabric of language and enhances reading and writing skills. Every child needs a conversational partner—someone who is gentle, affectionate, open-minded, curious, patient, and relaxed.

We all talk *to* our children every day: "Put your coat on," "Don't forget your lunch," "Wipe your shoes," "Take your bath," "Turn off the television," "Go to bed," etc. The great need is talking *with* children. This can include the following:

1. Converse with your children at the table. 2. Ask questions about their day-to-day activities. And share your own life experiences with your children. 3. Read aloud to your children and talk to them about the words and pictures. 4. Seek your child's opinion about issues — clothing, food, entertainment. 5. Encourage your child to enlarge on one- or two-word statements. 6. Provide options for your children when a decision has to be made. Ask them to give their reasons. 7. Invite your children to share in planning vacations. 8. Arrange for your preschoolers to play near you so you can converse with them about their play. 9. Ask your children to explain their pictures as they draw. Play verbal word games with your children using riddles, rhymes, synonyms, etc. 10. Name and identify unfamiliar objects or concepts as you read.[12]

Let me remind you again that children spell love t-i-m-e.

---

[1] Donald M. Joy, *Childhood Education in the Church*, ed. by Roy B. Zuck and Robert E. Clark (Chicago: Moody Press, 1975), p. 17.

[2] Ellen G. White, *Child Guidance*, p. 23.

[3] Joy, p. 17.

[4] David Heller, *Talking to Your Child About God* (Toronto: Bantam Books, 1988), pp. 157, 158.

[5] Adapted from Norman Wakefield, "Children and Their Theological Concepts," in *Childhood Education in the Church*, p. 130.

[6] Ellen G. White, *The Desire of Ages*, pp. 515, 69.

[7] Wakefield, p. 123.

[8] Adapted from V. Gilbert Beers, "Teaching Theological Concepts to Children," in *Childhood Education in the Church*, p. 142; Dolores Rowen, *Ways to Help Them Learn* (Glendale, Calif.: International Center for Learning, 1972), pp. 17-58.

[9] *U.S. News & World Report*, May 17, 1982.

[10] "Here's a Room Full of Success," Boston *Globe*, June 21, 1982, p. 6.

[11] Harvey S. Wiener, *Talk With Your Child* (New York: Penguin Books, 1988), p. 7.

[12] Adapted from Wiener, pp. 5-11.

Chapter 6

The Nature
and Needs of Adolescents

I am frightened and forlorn when I look at the youth of today. When I was a boy we were taught to respect our elders, and when I look at today's youth I wonder what is going to happen to the next generation."[1] Does this sound familiar? Actually, they are the words of the great Greek thinker Hesiod, who lived about 800 B.C. Adolescence has been called "a no-man's land." It identifies the dangerous passage between childhood and adulthood.

One factor complicating the teen years in our society is the lengthened time from adolescence to adulthood. One hundred years ago the average girl did not menstruate until she was 16 or 17 years of age. Now the average age is 12 or 13. The wide gap between physical maturity and emotional maturity has greatly increased the pressure on both parents and youth. The time spent in school further lengthens adolescence. Now the average young person will graduate from high school at about 18 years of age, and if he or she chooses to go on to college, it means another four or five years. The long transition from childhood to adulthood complicates matters for both youth and their parents. Adolescence begins at puberty, and puberty is "a biological event." It is a time of life that brings dramatic and sometimes painful changes. A glance at our society today reveals the acute nature of the problem—street gangs, substance abuse, teen pregnancies, violence, etc.

The adolescent, faced with a growing relationship to the outer world, begins breaking his or her dependence on parents. The Bible describes it this way: "For this reason a man will leave his father and mother" (Gen. 2:24, NIV). Adolescence is the time the "leaving" begins. Teenagers ask challenging questions: "Who am I in relation to the world?" "What am I going to do with my life?" "What are *my* values?" "What do *I* believe?" "What philosophy is worthwhile for *me?*" "What about religion?" "Are Mom and Dad right in their Seventh-day Adventist beliefs?"

An important part of the maturing process is intellectual growth. Earliteens find themselves in possession of new mental powers such as formal operational thought. Able to think systematically and more abstractly, they are more flexible in their reasoning. Their increased vocabulary aids them in problem solving, thus enabling them to reason in an almost scientific manner. And they look at all possible solutions to a problem.

I remember when I was 16 years of age and living with a great-aunt. She was easy to talk to and a good listener. We spent hours "arguing" about life, religion, and philosophy. Anyone hearing my comments would have been certain that I was headed for atheism. But with her keen insight into adolescence she knew that I was really "vocalizing my confusion." Her kind listening manner helped me to hammer out my own beliefs. The adolescent is constantly testing parents and teachers and trying out various roles. Teens also need limits. Early and middle teens usually have immature judgment. In their hearts they want parents and teachers to be firm and to clearly define acceptable behavior—with kindness, of course.

Peer Pressure

Why are teens so eager for acceptance by their peer group? During the teen years the pendulum of loyalties swings away from parents to those of similar age. It is natural for the teenager to want to cut the apron strings. Wise parents and teachers will help them do this. Every child needs two things—"roots and wings." As teens associate with one another they will often say to each other, "I feel the same as you do." And so adolescents find safety in numbers. They look for confidants. One of the most important concerns for teenagers is "What will my friends think of me?" And when parents try to enforce rules, teens will protest, "Everybody is doing it." Membership in a group gives the teenager status, companionship, security, and acceptance. Friends provide sounding boards and safety.

Teenagers are extremely self-conscious. How well I remember the time I spent in front of a mirror at 14 years of age. I worried about my pimples and my long nose. As I battled my rebellious hair, vaseline was the only thing I could afford. We tend to forget what it was like. Do you recall the euphoria you felt when you became a special friend of a certain girl or boy, or when you sensed you were accepted as a part of the group? When an adolescent encounters rejection, he or she has violent mood swings. Haim G. Ginott describes the timespan well: "Adolescence is a period of curative madness, in which every teenager has to remake his personality. He has to free himself from childhood ties with parents, establish new identifications with peers, and find his own identity."[2]

ADOLESCENCE: A CONTINUUM

Adolescence is a slow, protracted process beginning at about 12 or 13 and lasting to the early 20s. The early adolescent, concerned with self in relation to the group, deals with (1) independence from parents, (2) developing a mature value system/philosophy toward life, (3) developing a mature sex role, and (4) making career and lifestyle choices. Later adolescent identity struggles with self in relation to society. Young people have to deal with (1) continued body changes, (2) peer group membership, (3) cognitive development, and (4) heterosexual interaction.

Increased autonomy and independence characterize later adolescence. During this period young people often move away from home. They will develop cognitive skills that allow for more personal freedom and problem-solving ability as well as a relatively stable and self-determined peer relationship and increasing self-regulatory skills. The noncollege student may face vocational choices and may experiment with various job roles before he or she settles into a lifetime vocation. Later, adolescents become increasingly aware of the values and constraints of society and culture. But they continue the "sorting process" as they examine various options. The extreme idealism of early adolescence will become more realistic and down to earth.

Parents can be a great help for their teens by just being available when needed. Being a good sounding board is vital to successful parenting. Parents who learn to listen with their hearts in a spirit of patience and understanding can be a stabilizing influence. But the overanxious, prying, or critical parent will alienate his or her teens.

SEXUALITY

Any discussion of adolescence would be incomplete

without some mention of two critical areas: sexuality and music. If we want to teach the Bible creatively, we must help them come to grips with these issues. Nature is not kind to teens in our Western culture. Early pubescence (11 to 13) and the long wait till marriage (20 to 25 on an average) put our youth under considerable sexual tension. The sexual drive of the average male peaks at around 18 years of age. And to compound the problem, our sensate culture glorifies unrestrained sex. As Pitirim A. Sorokin, a Harvard sociologist, says, "The sex drive is now declared to be the most vital mainspring of human behavior. In the name of science, its fullest satisfaction is urged as a necessary condition of man's health and happiness. . . . Sexual chastity is ridiculed as a prudish superstition. . . . Our civilization has become so preoccupied with sex that it now oozes from all pores of American life."[3]

It would be nice if we could declare a sexual moratorium during the teen years or "put a dam on the flow of life," but that is simply impossible. Kathleen McCoy estimates that about half of the total U.S. teen population are sexually active. "The average teenager begins sexual activity at age 16. By age 19, only 20 percent of males and 33 percent of females have not had sexual intercourse."[4] Christian young people who have higher moral standards often find themselves socially isolated in the public school system because of their "prudish ways."

But Seventh-day Adventist youth are different, aren't they? Well, yes and no. They are human and have the same drives as everyone else, and they find themselves exposed to the sexual stimulation of society. In spite of Christian parents, our parochial school system, our Sabbath schools, and family worship, many of our youth succumb to temptation and engage in premarital sex. (According to the Valuegenesis report, 27 percent of twelfth graders have had sexual intercourse at least once.[5] The majority of our students felt the need for more sex education.[6])

It is extremely clear that if teens do not receive warmth and acceptance at home, they will surely find it among their peers. Our young people are looking for sensible answers. They want to hear about sexuality in a healthy way. If parents and teachers don't provide sexual education, young people will get it from television, the playground, and the street. Teenagers rarely come to parents or teachers on their own for information. In a recent study Kinsey reported that only 5 percent of teenage boys would feel free to talk to their fathers about sexuality. Mothers scored better — 10 percent — but teachers only 1 percent. The majority would prefer to get their information from a doctor or nurse (44 percent) or a friend (19 percent).[7] Fourteen-year-old Isabell said, "I can't talk to Mom about sex, and I'm surely not going to go to my father. So where do I learn?" Far too many Seventh-day Adventist homes have an unbroken code: "We don't talk about such things. Here's a book." Ginott says, "Sex education is now needed to serve as an antidote to sex propaganda. Society can no longer passively permit the street and the screen to set its sex standards."[8] Young people need two things: sex education and values. The home, the school, and the church must be responsible for them.

Adults should speak of sexuality as God's wonderful gift to the human family. What an adolescent really wants is to come to terms with his or her sexuality on an emotional level. So our challenge as parents and teachers is to communicate values — God's values and philosophy. The love narratives about Isaac and Rebecca, Jacob and Rachel, Ruth and Boaz, Joseph and Mary provide marvelous opportunities for idealizing love and marriage. We should provide forums for discussing these issues. Young people should have the opportunity to explore them in a wholesome, spiritual way. (See chapter 12, p. 99.)

TEENS AND MUSIC

Recently some students in a sixth-grade music class asked their teacher about the meaning of the lyrics in some rock music. The 23-year-old teacher tried to explain tactfully what they meant. The next day the principal of the school received several telephone calls from irate parents because the teacher was talking about satanism and necrophilia with their children.

These parents, like many Seventh-day Adventists, have no idea what some rock lyrics are communicating to their children. "Today's rock music extols everything from rape, incest, and homosexuality to sadomasochism and bestiality. . . . Other lyrics glamorize drug and alcohol use, and glorify death and violent rebellion." [9]

Are Christian young people and Seventh-day Adventist youth in particular listening to rock? If you have been around our youth at all, you are well aware that the majority of them have regular exposure to it. We should ask ourselves: "Why are our children listening to these songs? What does this tell us about our children? Why are so many addicted?" It is true that youth use music and clothes to distinguish themselves from their parents. And independence from parents at this age is normal. Bruno Bettelheim suggests that addiction "to a certain kind of music or to a certain musical group . . . means there is a gap in his life he's trying to fill. Many teenagers turn up the hi-fi full blast to blast other thoughts out of their heads. It is a way of getting away from troubling feelings or to fill a void. It is similar to an addiction to drugs. People become addicted, not because drugs are around, but because of emptiness. If everything in a young person's life is in order, then the media will have very little influence." [10] Here is a tremendous challenge to Christian parents and teachers! Could it be that Christ is not filling the "gap" in their lives? Are rules the answer? I think not. I like Alden Thompson's way of putting it: that we can better describe the Bible and the writings of Ellen White as a "casebook" rather than a "codebook." [11] What better place to examine and probe musical issues than at home, in Bible class, or in Sabbath school classes? Why not read some of the lyrics and talk about their effect? Ask such questions as "What builds faith and why?" "What destroys faith and why?" Lead the class to seek for principles rather than just accepting edicts.

Developmentally, teenagers need spontaneity and a way of self-expression. Music can be fun as well as winsome, can contribute to a spiritual high without being like a mood-altering drug. It can be restful, relaxing, or joyful, exuberant, and exciting. But let us not insist on everyone thinking the same, or interpreting the Bible or the writings of Ellen White in an identical manner. Instead, let us allow for cultural and age differences, and above all, let us listen to the voice of the Spirit. "Great principles have been laid down in His Word, which are sufficient to guide us in our Christian walk." [12] To those who yield themselves to God, the Holy Spirit will give clear discernment. [13]

Nathan Pusey, former president of Harvard University, reportedly said that students are looking for a flag to follow, a song to sing, and a creed to believe. What a challenge to parents, Bible teachers, and pastors! "With such an army of workers as our youth, rightly trained, might furnish, how soon the message of a crucified, risen, and soon-coming Saviour might be carried to the whole world!" [14]

[1] John Bradshaw, "The Eight Stages of Man," public television lecture.

[2] Haim G. Ginott, *Between Parent and Teenager* (New York: Avon Books, 1969), p. 25.

[3] Pitirim A. Sorokin, *The American Sex Revolution* (Boston: Porter Sargent Publisher, 1956), pp. 17, 19, 25.

[4] Kathleen McCoy, *Coping With Teenage Depression* (New York: New American Library, 1985), p. 207.

[5] *Valuegenesis Report III*, p. 20.

[6] *Valuegenesis Report I*, p. 29.

[7] *The Kinsey Institute New Report on Sex* (New York: St. Martin's Press, 1990), p. 21.

[8] Ginott, p. 167.

[9] Peggy Mann, "How Shock Rock Harms Our Kids," in *Reader's Digest*, July 1988, p. 101.

[10] Bruno Bettelheim, "TV Stereotypes 'Devastating' to Young Minds," *U.S. News & World Report*, Oct. 28, 1985, p. 55.

[11] See Alden Thompson, *Inspiration* (Hagerstown, Md.: Review and Herald Pub. Assn., 1991), pp. 98-109.

[12] Ellen G. White, *Testimonies*, vol. 3, p. 523.

[13] ——, *The Desire of Ages*, p. 456, and *Selected Messages*, book 2, p. 274.

[14] ——, *Education*, p. 271.

Chapter 7

The Nature
and Needs of Adults

What do you see when you view a group of adults? Drastic variety. Adults differ greatly from each other. A typical adult class many include young adults at the peak of their vigor physically and mentally; middle adults with a touch of gray here and there; and senior adults coping with retirement and diminished activity. They may represent a wide range of ethnic backgrounds, socioeconomic levels, and sharply contrasting life experiences and educational levels. The purpose of this chapter is to help Bible teachers recognize the vast differences in adults, to help them understand the learning characteristics of the various age levels, and then to minister to their varying needs. Remember, learning is a lifelong experience.

I enjoy teaching adults because they are so rich in experience. They come to a class with such a wide variety of temperaments, skills, abilities, and backgrounds. Each one is unique and gifted by God with a broad spectrum of talents and insights. Some are vocal and aggressive while others are timid and pensive. But the richness of the adult years adds great potential for class interaction. Our task is to draw them out so that everyone can share their experiences.

YOUNG ADULTS

Lois grew up in a single-parent family. Her father died when she was 4 years old, and her mother struggled to provide for two children and to keep them in church school. Finally Lois went off to boarding academy, but she was unhappy. She deeply resented the restrictions. During her senior year the school expelled her. In high school she started dancing lessons and soon grew weary of Sabbath school and church. She went on to college, took a degree in sociology, and married a high school sweetheart. A few years later they had their first child. When little Tommy was about 3 years of age Lois felt deeply her responsibility to guide him in the right way, and she wanted him to grow up believing in God. Remembering her childhood experience in Sabbath school and the positive memories of cradle roll and kindergarten, she looked up the address of the Adventist church and took Tommy to cradle roll. The other mothers were friendly. Tommy greatly enjoyed Sabbath school. Someone invited her to attend an adult class. The subject of the lesson study was the book of Ezekiel, and the teacher, an elder in the church, was primarily concerned with some of the more technical aspects of the book. Lois attended a few times and then concluded that it did not meet her needs. Eventually she decided to take Tommy to a Sunday school just two blocks down the road from where they lived.

What was the problem here? Where did our church fail? One thing is certain—Sabbath school teachers need to understand the developmental needs of young adults and teach to meet those needs. Whenever possible the Sabbath school should place young adults in a class with other young adults. According to Robert Havighurst, some of the developmental tasks for young adults are "(1) completing or continuing education, (2) selecting a mate, (3) learning to live with a marriage partner, (4) starting a family, (5) rearing children, (6) managing a home, (7) getting started in an occupation, (8) taking on civic responsibility, and (9) finding a congenial social group." [1]

A great hemorrhage is taking place in our church — the loss of young adults 18 to 30 years of age. Thousands are barely clinging to the church. Sabbath school teachers have an enormous privilege and responsibility as young people search for meaning in life. We must base our ministry on their needs.

Frank teaches a class of young adults. He recognizes that most of them have small children, so he looks for material that will be particularly helpful to parents. Often he quotes from and recommends various books on child development and shares his own experiences as well as those of others. Indeed, Frank holds the interest of his learners. They have developed a good social program, and his class is always crowded. Note the words of Ellen White: "Teachers are needed who are able to deal wisely with the different phases of character." [2]

MIDDLE ADULTS

The house never seemed so big. The excitement of the wedding was over, and the next morning Ken and Martha sat together at the breakfast table. Ken looked at Martha, her head covered with curlers. She had gained weight, had lost her youthful figure, and looked all of her 46 years. They both sat there glumly because they had argued the night before over some financial matters. After he left for work she sat down in her favorite chair and wondered what the future held. She admitted to herself that their marriage had become a bore and that the closeness they once enjoyed had gone. Ken's job often took him away on business trips, and she wondered if he would resist the temptations that were bound to come. And their spiritual life had become perfunctory.

The next Sabbath they were sitting together in class. The topic of the quarter's study was the book of Proverbs, and the current lesson dealt with King Solomon and his temptations. Jerry, the Sabbath school teacher, was well acquainted with all of his members. He tried to bring things out to help them in their everyday living. Most of the class were middle-aged. They had an interesting discussion on Solomon's failure to grow as a Christian, his lavish lifestyle, and his selfish splurges. The discussion at one point touched on the problems that people face in middle-age. The texts and the discussion seemed to be just what Ken and Martha needed. That night as they were lying in bed together she unburdened her heart. They talked about middle-age and some of its pitfalls. "You are right," Ken said. "Middle-age does pose real problems, especially when children leave. We have placed our affections and thoughts upon our children, and now they are gone and we are alone."

"Yes, we must change our thinking now and seek that closeness we once enjoyed," Martha replied.

One of the developmental tasks of middle-age is to become involved in church, civic, and social responsibilities. Middle-age often gives more freedom to devote to creative activity. It brings increased leisure time and more financial resources to manage. The middle-aged person has years of experience in making decisions, so the period should be one of the most productive times of life.

OLDER ADULTS

Justice Brennan of the United States Supreme Court (who was in his 80s) announced his retirement. At a press conference following his announcement, a journalist asked Brennan if he had found it more difficult to analyze complex legal briefs lately. He replied that his powers of concentration and analysis had not diminished. Senior citizens across the country read his comment and took heart. One man said, "Well, the body may be wearing out, but I am determined to keep my mind young by keeping it active." The happiest seniors are those who continue to let life challenge them.

Many people retire when they are at the zenith of their ability to contribute. As John Bradshaw says: "We retire people right when they 'hit wisdom.'"[3] Old age does have its challenges. Erik Erikson identifies the crisis of old age as "ego integrity versus despair." And how do we avoid despair? We need to own life from beginning to end. Denial is the pitfall. Someone asked Plato whether life gets hard at the end. He said, "Well, if it was hard in the beginning and the middle, it will probably be hard in the end." An older person who has a sense of hope, a trust in God, and a sense of purpose, competence, and of love and caring, can say, "It's OK." In most other cultures of the world people don't retire—they just keep on keeping on. Our challenge as Bible teachers is to nurture them, and enlist them.

Here are some guidelines for teaching seniors: 1. Help them to accept the aging process and develop faith to cope with illness, loneliness, financial stresses, and the fear of death and dying. 2. Tell about people who have made great contributions to the church and to society in old age. 3. Emphasize our blessed hope—the soon coming of Jesus and heaven. 4. Use the discussion method. Make Bible class a time for sharing and caring.

SINGLE ADULTS

"More than 28 percent of the church is comprised of unmarried adults over the age of 25."[4] Single adults come under three headings—the never married, the widowed, and the divorced. Then we have the separated who also are in a definite sense single.

The Seventh-day Adventist Church has neglected singles as a group. (The situation is changing at the present time.) The problem is a social attitude that regards unmarried people as "failures." As Christians we must recognize the legitimacy of being unmarried. Unfortunately we fail to see the unwed state as a viable condition of life. And so many of our single members suffer loneliness and rejection. We should view them as normal people who have chosen to be single.

What can the church do to integrate this important segment into the body better? Many of our congregations are now organizing single ministries. Reaching out to other singles in the community is a wonderful missionary opportunity. It can be done through music, recreation, and Bible discussion groups.

Some years ago I was a pastor of a suburban church. As I analyzed my church membership I noticed a large number of single women members. Many of them were professional or business persons. We organized a special Sabbath school class for them, selecting a teacher who was an outstanding and successful woman in the community who also happened to be unmarried. It was amazing to see the class grow and to watch them take on projects. People who have much in common will understand and support each other when brought together in a Bible study group. This class proved to be a real blessing to them and to the church as a whole.

ADULT LEARNING CHARACTERISTICS

Adult learning is different from childhood learning. You may tell children that they should memorize the multiplication table because they will need the knowledge all through life, and they will dutifully do so—usually. Not so adults. Ask adults to memorize verses of Scripture, and they are very apt to procrastinate. Adults are "problem centered" in their learning orientation. Living in a rough-and-tumble world, they will not usually apply themselves to absorbing a subject unless they feel convinced that it will immediately benefit them. They will respond: "What does the Bible say that will help me with the problems that I am facing today? I do not want to wait until next week or next month for answers."

Older adults often feel insecure in a formal class situation. I have often overheard someone say, "I'm afraid I will be asked a question and won't know the answer." Every teacher of adults needs to keep the following dictum in mind: *Adults change slowly.* Teachers must adapt their teaching to the needs of the class members.

Our challenge is to lead adults into lifelong learning. Please note the following summary of adult educational principles: 1. Adults do maintain the ability to learn. 2. They are a highly diversified group of individuals with widely differing preferences, needs, backgrounds, and skills. 3. Every adult experiences a gradual decline in physical and sensory capabilities. 4. Experience is a major resource in learning situations. 5. Self-concept moves from dependency to independence as individuals grow in responsibility, experience, and confidence. 6. And finally, adults tend to be life-centered in their orientation to learning.

As I consider the aging process I recall the words of Robert Browning that it is the period of life "for which the first was made."

---

[1] *Adult Education in the Church*, ed. by Roy B. Zuck and Gene A. Getz (Chicago: Moody Press, 1970), pp. 37, 38.

[2] Ellen G. White, *Counsels to Parents and Teachers*, p. 180.

[3] Bradshaw, "Eight Stages of Man."

[4] Blake Hall, "Of Duchesses and Jerkwater Dukes," *Adventist Review*, Nov. 21, 1991, pp. 14, 15.

Encouragement:
The Key to
Self-worth and Motivation

B etty? Oh, she works hard, but she's just an average student. She certainly doesn't measure up to her older sister in any way." Unfortunately the girl happened to overhear her math teacher's remark as the woman was visiting at lunch with another faculty member at an Adventist day academy. The girl's eyes brimmed with tears as she turned away. *I studied three hours for that algebra test and end up with a C. Oh, what's the use!* Bonnie, her older sister, was a superior student, popular, and extremely attractive. She got the smiles, nods, and the accolades, but Betty couldn't seem to excel in anything. Her problem? She was just average—freckles, a bit overweight, and rather shy. Gradually she lost interest in school and began spending much of her time with friends who accepted her just as she was. Becoming rebellious, she lost all interest in religious things. "What's wrong with Betty?" parents and teachers asked.

Hero worship is the hallmark of our culture. The media (and many parents and teachers) play up the beautiful and the intelligent. Betty had often heard her parents say, "Average is not good enough. Study harder if you want to amount to something." GPA is the magic word in academia. "Nursing school, physical therapy? Perhaps you should consider a vocational school." Someone overheard Betty say to a friend: "I don't count in this school or in this church because I'm not a very good student."

Most negative behavior in our society stems from discouragement. Why should I devote a chapter in this book to encouragement and self-worth? Because, in my opinion, it is the key to a productive, full life of service. If you would teach the Bible creatively, you must learn the art of encouragement. "Encourage one another and build each other up. . . . Encourage the timid, help the weak" (1 Thess. 5:11-14, NIV). Pray for the gift of encouraging (Rom. 12:8).

What do we mean by "self-worth"? Really how people feel about themselves represents their overall judgment about themselves as a person. Dorothy Corkille Briggs, in her valuable book *Your Child's Self-esteem*, says, "*High self-esteem is not a noisy conceit.* It is a quiet sense of self respect, a feeling of self-worth. . . . With high self-esteem you don't waste time and energy impressing others; you already know you have value. . . . Your child's judgment of himself influences the kinds of friends he chooses, how he gets along with others, the kind of person he marries, and how productive he will be. It affects his creativity, integrity, stability, and even whether he will be a leader or a follower. His feelings of self-worth form the core of his personality and determine the use he makes of his aptitudes and abilities. . . . In fact, *self-esteem is the mainspring that slates every child for success or failure as a human being* . . . [and] the mainspring for motivation"[1]

A newborn has no sense of self as a person. As time

goes on, however, his or her mind absorbs thousands of little impressions. Father bounces little Charles on his knee, and with a big smile says, "He's all boy." Sue hears her grandmother say, "Isn't she a doll?" Dan listens to his mother complain, "He just never sits still. I don't know what I'm going to do with him. He drives me up the wall!"

Pete's father demands of him, "Why are you so clumsy and so uncoordinated?" Later his mother says, "You're too little, let Mother do it." What is Pete to conclude?

To a child, parents are "psychological mirrors." He or she accepts uncritically parental evaluation. Children value themselves to the degree that they are valued.[2]

If the balance of input tends toward the positive, a child's self-image will be healthy even though the youngster has experienced the normal ups and downs of childhood. Negative experiences will leave a child with a bad self-image. Now identify which of the following statements reflect a healthy self-worth and which would indicate a poor sense of self: 1. I am stronger than you are. 2. I'm no good at games. 3. I like school. 4. Let me do it. 5. I'm ugly. 6. Let me help.

When Pete is 12 or 13 years of age and someone invites him to a party, he may hang back and make excuses about not getting involved in the games. Or he could try to be the life of the party and do lots of bragging. Perhaps he may even become aggressive and domineering. All of these behaviors could reflect a poor sense of personal worth. "Usually, the worse the child's behavior, the greater his cry for approval."[3]

Kenneth is always bragging and pushing the smaller children around. Shorter than the others, he masks his feelings of inferiority by trying to "look good." Such compensatory behavior is usually a dead giveaway to a poor sense of self-worth. I remember Larry, who was short and skinny but had a brilliant mind. Making top grades, he enjoyed vexing the other children who were average or below average. He bragged about his grades and, of course, was "teacher's pet."

SUGGESTIONS

James Dobson offers some pertinent suggestions for helping children develop a healthy self-respect: 1. Help your child compensate. Enable him to find his or her natural abilities and then capitalize on them. 2. Help your child compete. Society puts value on beauty, brawn, and brains. Assist your child in becoming as attractive as possible, but also teach him or her about the true values — love, kindness, integrity, truthfulness, and devotion to God. 3. Discipline with respect. Be careful about corporal punishment. 4. Avoid overprotection. Help children to make as many choices on their own as possible.[4]

The person who encourages will always value the child as he or she is. Such an individual will show faith in the child and enable the child to believe in himself or herself. "I like the way you handled that." "Knowing you, I know you can do it." Then the adult will recognize a job well done. "You did a good job, George. Thank you very much." Many failing children have fallen into a "learned helplessness." They realize that we classify them as failures, so they live up to our expectations.

Encourage the development of skills sequentially and psychologically paced to permit success. Focus on the strengths and assets. And, of course, the most important thing is a religious faith. Children who truly believe in their hearts that God sent Jesus to be their Saviour and that Jesus died for them will see themselves as God sees them — as of enormous value. God gives us unconditional love. We must do the same to others.

Deborah Mowray gives some helpful suggestions for the classroom. (You can also adapt the following for Sabbath school or home.)

1. Design a special bulletin board. Feature a new student weekly. Secure a picture of the child, list his/her age, birth date, favorite sport, favorite food, names of his/her brothers and sisters, where he/she lives, and some interesting facts about his/her family.

2. "I am thumb-body special." With a paper and ink pad have students make their thumbprint at the top of the page. Explain that no two people in the world have the same thumbprint.

3. "I am special because I am *me*." "Write six things about yourself that you would never want to lose, trade, or give away."

4. "I do some things purr . . . fectly well." Talk about the courage it takes to admit we don't know some things. Discuss the word "skills." Ask students to list at least four skills they know they have.

5. "We're all different." Ask the students to think of three things that make them different from other people.

THE POWER OF AFFIRMATION

Miss Jones was a teacher of seventh-graders in a rural community. One day when the students had done considerable criticism and bickering, she thought of a possible solution. "Instead of doing social studies during this next hour," she said, "I want you to do something entirely different. List the names of each person in our class and leave room to write a paragraph under each name. Now, in the space under each name please write two or three sentences listing the nice things that you like about each person."

At first the students seemed a bit shocked, but finally they got down to business and seemed to enjoy what they were doing. That night she stayed up until midnight compiling the results. She wrote the name of each of the 18 students at the top of a sheet of paper and then listed all of the nice things that others had written about that individual. The next morning she gave each student a list of the good comments made by their peers. As the students read their papers total silence filled the room. Then came smiles and handshakes and hugs. The exercise brought a lasting change in the social relationships. Miss Jones repeated the exercise every year after that.

Ten years later Miss Jones retired. Some of her former students got together and planned a farewell for her. The emcee asked each person present—and more than one hundred came—to say the one thing that he or she remembered most about Miss Jones. The first to speak was a tall, lanky truck driver. He reached for his wallet, pulled out a crumpled piece of paper, and held it up. "Do you remember when we were asked to write nice things about each other? I still carry this list of the things that my peers liked about me. I read it every once in a while, especially when I get down in the dumps." With that he sat down. Several others dug into purses and wallets and brought out rumpled pieces of paper. Yes, the same list. An older woman stood and said, "I am George Wallace's mother. As you know, he was killed in Vietnam. The government sent me his personal effects, and in his wallet I found this paper, his list of good things his fellow students had written about him. It obviously had been read many times, and he had it with him when he died." She sat down, and the only sound in the room was Miss Jones weeping. Strong young men reached for handkerchiefs to wipe their eyes. Then the emcee said with a trembling voice as he faced their teacher. "You taught us many good things, but the greatest lesson was the power of loving affirmation."

Don Dinkmeyer and Rudolf Dreikurs talk about the power of encouragement: "The significance of encouragement is far too little recognized. . . . So crucial is the factor of encouragement that once its significance is recognized, it may actually revolutionize educational procedures in our families and in our schools. For this reason, the process of encouragement must be carefully and thoroughly explored and our teachers, in particular, acquainted with the full scope of this highly powerful corrective technique."[5]

---

[1] Dorothy Corkille Briggs, *Your Child's Self-esteem* (Garden City, New York: Doubleday and Company, Inc., 1970), p. 3.

[2] *Ibid.*, pp. 9-57.

[3] *Ibid.*, p. 34.

[4] Condensed from James Dobson, *Hide or Seek*, pp. 47-137.

[5] Dinkmeyer and Dreikurs, pp. 1, 3, 4.

Chapter 9

Learning About Learning

Have you ever tried to tell someone how to tie a necktie? Do it sometime. You will quickly learn the chief weakness of the "telling" method of education. How did you learn to tie your shoes? Someone probably demonstrated the procedure, then helped you step by step. Then you practiced, practiced, and practiced.

When I was about 10 years old I remember how desperately I wanted to learn to ride a bicycle. First, I observed carefully how people rode, and thought how it looked so easy. I reasoned that if I could learn to balance first, that would be a good beginning. So I used the bicycle as a scooter—I stood with one foot on the pedal, and with the other I pushed myself along. After several tumbles I finally acquired the balancing skill. Then one day I got up my courage and swung my right leg over the seat and started on my way with both feet on the pedals. What euphoria! What exhilaration! (It was an example of sequential learning.) Of course, I had spills and bruises (negative reinforcement), but something impelled me to keep on (intrinsic motivation), and my friends encouraged me (extrinsic motivation). Fewer tumbles and more successes occurred as the days went by (positive reinforcement).

Let us consider a few of the most important principles of teaching learning. How does learning occur? How can teachers become "learning enablers"? Paul wrote to young Timothy that overseers of the church should be "able to teach" (1 Tim. 3:2, NIV). The Bible contains a number of clues as to methodology all through it. David prays, "Show me your ways, O Lord, teach me your paths; guide me in your truth and teach me. . . . Good and upright is the Lord; therefore he instructs sinners in his ways" (Ps. 25:4-8, NIV). Notice some key words here: God "shows," "guides," and "instructs" as He teaches. Such words imply that teaching is more than "telling." Bible teachers are to be learning guides. Learners cannot be passive—they must be involved in the process. Ellen White says that educators should "call out the ability and powers of the student, instead of constantly endeavoring to impart instruction."[1] She speaks of using the very best methods and even adopting new methods in educating our youth.[2]

LEARNING THEORY

What is learning? I have discovered that it's difficult to define. Howard L. Kingsley and Ralph Garry suggest that learning alters behavior. "Learning, then, is the process by which an organism, in satisfying its motivations, adapts or adjusts to a situation in which it must modify its behavior in order to overcome obstacles or barriers." They continue to say that *"learning is the process by which behavior (in the broader sense) is originated or changed through practice or training."*[3] In short, then, learning is change . . . response . . . satisfaction—all are a part of the whole. For us, learning includes change that moves us closer to Christ and thus closer to a Godlike character. Now, teaching: what is it? I like Richard C. Sprinthall and Norman A. Sprinthall's definition: "Teaching is the management of instruction."[4]

For centuries people believed that rote memorization was the highest form of learning. Never mind that most usually did not understand the implications of what they were learning. It was enough to repeat it. During the 1960s researchers did a survey in terms of teacher talk versus student talk. They found that teachers did about 70 percent of all talking in the classroom — a lot of it simply the asking of questions. And when the researchers looked at the questions, they discovered that around 80 percent of all questions called for responses based on rote memory. The teacher typically asked about two questions per minute, and the student's response was almost exclusively short replies to them. Any kind of interaction between student and teacher was virtually nonexistent. So things haven't changed much in spite of all the modern theory.[5]

Educators have come up with many theories of how to teach learning, but no single theory probes its depth. It seems to me that teaching is more of an art than an exact science. Yet educational psychology has given us some valuable insights into the teaching-learning process.

Piaget reportedly said that if you tell children something, they will soon forget it. But if you allow them to discover it for themselves, they will probably remember it for the rest of their lives. The challenge is to provide conditions in which such discovery can happen. I have used an exercise in which I asked the children to "catch the teacher" in a mistake. It is both fun and leads to discovery by helping children to learn to listen critically and to reason on higher cognitive levels. Of course, it is not the only form of learning, but the discovery method is probably our most powerful device in teaching the Bible. Yes, I know it takes time and demands creativity, imagination, and flexibility. And we recognize that students need some knowledge of the subject to use this method.

TRANSFER

One of our most important goals in Bible teaching is to help students apply what they learn in Bible class to life situations. Learning theorists tell us that transfer is really the key to classroom learning. It takes place when learning task A helps us to learn task B. When we discover how to add and subtract, it prepares us to monitor our checkbooks. Memorizing the Ten Commandments is important—but obviously not enough. Our challenge is to simulate situations in which learners see how principles apply to everyday life. For example, you trigger a lively discussion on a thought-provoking question. As the class discusses the issue, it ignites lots of intellectual sparks, and the learners begin to make discoveries. In my opinion, memorizing Bible verses has little value unless the students learn to generalize and develop the ability to transfer the principles they acquire into life experiences.

Mr. Gordon teaches first-grade Bible class. A key verse is "Be kind one to another." The children repeated the verse in unison about four times before talking about its meaning. He asked the learners to name three persons or animals that need kindness. Then he raised such questions as "Why should we be kind?" "How will this help you?" "How will it make Jesus feel?"

Mr. Knauft teaches twelfth-grade Bible and had his students write a paper on Daniel 2 showing how they would use this story to help a neighbor friend who believed that the Bible is mostly folklore. The question is "How does a knowledge of Bible prophecy help substantiate faith in the Bible as the Word of God?" This is what we mean by transfer.

LEVELS OF LEARNING

Facts are the building blocks of learning. God has chosen to reveal Himself in the Bible through words — factual information. Students need to know cognitively facts about Jesus, His teaching, and His life, death, and resurrection. They must grasp the doctrinal teachings of the Seventh-day Adventist Church. But learning must go beyond factual understanding to be meaningful. Bible facts, like bricks in a building, must be organized in a meaningful way to convey ideas and concepts.

The restatement-generalization level of learning presents real challenges. Seventh-grade teacher Georgia asked her class, "Can you give me the names of the two disciples who dishonored Jesus, one by denying Him and the other by betraying Him?" They responded: "Peter denied his Lord and Judas betrayed Him." Then their teacher continued, "Both afterward regretted their actions. What was the difference in their response?" This interchange demands not only a factual knowledge of the story but also asks for a generalization.

A higher level of learning is implication-application. Our seventh-grade teacher goes to the chalkboard and writes the word "Peter" at the head of one column and "Judas" at the other. She asks, "How would you characterize Peter's repentance?" The class responds: "Peter's repentance was genuine, heartfelt, specific, permanent, and motivated by love."

"And how would you describe Judas' repentance?" Response: "Judas' repentance was motivated by fear, it was insincere, it was not based on love, and it led to his suicide."

"Now," our teacher continues, "what can we learn from these stories about the nature of repentance? Please take a sheet of paper and write down three lessons that you have learned about the nature of repentance. As you write, consider what it feels like to be betrayed or denied. How do you think Jesus felt about His two disciples? Is it hard for you to forgive those who deny and reject you?"

Here we have an example of the implication-application level of learning. The writing exercise leads the students to examine their own feelings and to identify the lessons that they can transfer to their own life experience.

MAKING LEARNING A JOY

It was my first time on the ski slopes in the western Cascades. I felt extremely clumsy with all of that gear—boots, clamps, ski poles, to say nothing of the multiple layers of clothing. As I watched the other skiers it looked so easy. Then I listened to the "pro." "Well," I said to myself, "I can't stop here." So up I went—up on the bunny tow with all the kids. Although I felt self-conscious, I noticed other adults just starting out too. All of us had lots of falls and laughs. My skis seemed determined to go in different directions. But finally I made it down the short slope without a fall. And it was fun! After two or three more trips to the ski area I graduated to the intermediate slope. Then—I will always remember the day—I came down the slope at a good clip right through the powder with snow flying. What a thrill—ecstasy! Yes, learning does have its rewards.

And what about the Bible? When George said to me, "I really never thought of it that way. Now I think I am beginning to understand righteousness by faith," he was experiencing the joy of learning the Bible. And more important—he was discovering Jesus as Friend and Saviour.

Are your students experiencing the pleasure of

learning? Are they making thrilling discoveries in the Word? Are they getting acquainted with Jesus? If they are, then Bible study will become a joy, and Bible class will be what it should be — the best class of the day.

---

[1] Ellen G. White, *Counsels on Sabbath School Work*, p. 166.

[2] *Ibid.*, pp. 11, 164.

[3] Howard L. Kingsley and Ralph Garry, *The Nature and Conditions of Learning* (Englewood Cliffs, N.J.: Prentice-Hall, 1946), pp. 9-12.

[4] Richard C. Sprinthall and Norman A. Sprinthall, *Educational Psychology: A Developmental Approach*, p. 253.

[5] *Ibid.*, p. 21.

Chapter 10

Speaking of Methods . . .

This job is going to take forever at this rate," my wife said. The weather was hot, and we were perspiring as we chipped away at dry rot in the floor of our trailer. It had been stored for years, and the floor was badly infested. "What we need is a circle saw. Without it we will be here all day," I commented. Finally we decided to pay the money, painful as it was. But with our brand-new Skilsaw we got the job done in short order. You guessed it—good teaching methods are like power tools. The right tools will greatly simplify fixing the brakes on your car, making bread, or even cleaning the house. We need the best methods and strategies to encourage thinking, reasoning, memorizing, and applying.

DEVELOPING A LESSON PLAN

Success in any endeavor depends upon careful planning, whether it be a meal, a garden, or a vacation. Recently we planned our retirement home and learned that what goes into the plan comes out in the house. Yes, careful planning pays off. The same principle holds true in planning for learning.

The first thing I do in preparing for a Bible study, or a formal teaching situation, is to determine the central truth or key point in the lesson. I take time to consider the lesson as a whole. Is there one idea that encompasses the entire lesson? The process is known as "synthesis" and helps me in selecting the proper teaching strategies and in choosing illustrations. It really "puts a handle on the lesson." Then I write the central truth or point in one sentence. John Sisemore says that it should be "a complete comprehensive statement that can be used, evaluated, and written out." [1]

With the key point in mind, I break the material down into subtopics. Often I state the central truth to my class at the beginning of the teaching session and then restate it at the conclusion.

Then I consider the life needs of my members. Perhaps I visualize Dan and Sue and their financial problems or I recall Ruth and her difficulties with her teenage children, etc. These needs of my class members—and I know them quite well—color my study and presentation. This principle holds true whether I am preparing to give a Bible study to one person, teach a Sabbath school class, or conduct a sixth-grade Bible class.

Have you ever sat in a Bible class in which the teacher, like a butterfly, seemed to flit aimlessly from one beautiful truth to another? It is much more satisfying when he or she has organized the material and the presentation moves in a straight line toward a specific educational objective. We might characterize this as "beeline teaching." "Before attempting to teach a subject, he [the teacher] should have a distinct plan in mind, and should know just what he desires to accomplish." [2]

A model I have found helpful in preparing to teach is to ask myself: 1. What do I want these learners to remember about this lesson? 2. How do I want them to feel about the lesson? 3. How do I want them to respond? What do I want them to do? 4. But the big question is What do I want these learners to be like after they have experienced the teaching session?

Most teachers have an aim, but aims need to be specific. Instead of saying "My aim today is to make better Christians," it is better to say, "As a result of this lesson I want my students to be more unselfish in their relationships in the home this coming week."

EARNING THE RIGHT TO TEACH

The teacher earns the right to teach when he or she secures the undivided attention of his or her students. We have all kinds of competition: a police car racing down the highway, a bird singing outside the window, the movement of chairs and tittering in the room. Your job as teacher is to bait the hook, to lure students' minds. Someone said that if you don't "strike oil" in the first 30 seconds of your class, you may as well stop boring. Try something like this: "Last night, just as we were getting ready to go to bed, we heard this terrible bang outside. It sounded like a gunshot. I rushed to the window, and lying on the pavement was . . ." Or "Let me tell you about the most embarrassing moment of my life . . ." Spend time planning a good introduction. Jesus was a master at getting attention. His favorite method was a brief, well-told story. Everyone will pay attention if it promises to fill a need. Your "attention device must relate to the lesson and lead directly into the central truth. It should be like a porch on a house: inviting but architecturally fitting with the rest of the house. . . . The transition to the lesson should be as smooth and natural as possible."[3] Let me share with you some of my favorite strategies for inductive Bible study.

SCRIPTURE SEARCH

The purpose of this exercise is to lead the class to examine carefully a specific passage. It would apply at a home Bible study, a Sabbath school class, or a formal teaching session in a twelfth-grade Bible class. "Please open your Bibles to such and such a text. Look for three steps to repentance. You have three minutes. Then share with a neighbor." This strategy leads the class to discoveries in the Word. The members articulate what they find to fellow class members, and this leads naturally into an exciting class discussion.

BIBLE PARAPHRASE

The following sample exercise would be appropriate for family worship, a Sabbath school class, or a seventh-grade Bible class. The lesson title is "The Guilty May Know Him." "Please read Romans 1:20 several times," you might begin. "Look at the context and think through the meaning of the passage. Underline the key words. Rewrite the verse in your own words. Then share your 'paraphrase' with the person next to you and discuss the meaning of the passage." Obviously, as someone reads, analyzes, and rewrites the verse, he or she will discover its meaning. Sharing the verse with a neighbor or the rest of the family will help to fasten the scripture in mind.

CRITICAL THINKING, CLASSIFYING, OR COMPARING

The object of this activity is to help students learn how to analyze, classify, and compare Scripture. Let's say the lesson topic is "Our Response to Conviction." Jacob and Peter responded to God's Spirit in different ways. In Jacob's prayer he said: "I will not let you go unless you bless me" (Gen. 32:26, NIV). Note the words of Peter: "When Simon Peter saw this, he fell at Jesus' knees and said, 'Go away from me, Lord; I am a sinful man!'" (Luke 5:8, NIV). Now have the class contrast the two responses to the work of the Holy Spirit.

The class provides the input, and the teacher writes the responses under the appropriate column: PETER and JACOB. One might ask: "What needs do these two men have in common? What are the differences? Contrast the circumstances." The teacher guides the discussion. This approach puts the burden directly on the learner. Everyone is involved in searching Scripture.

CASE STUDY

Scripture passage: 2 Chronicles 24. The title of the lesson is "A Good Beginning but a Sad Ending." Allow five minutes to review the story of Joash. Ask the class to look for clues as to why this king who started so well ended so sadly. Have them write one lesson they could apply to their lives and then share with a neighbor. The last 30 minutes of the period could be spent in discussing the issues. I always prepare five or six good discussion questions written out on a chalkboard ahead of time.

RESOLVING A CONFLICT

Your lesson title is "Diet and Health." You could begin your discussion as follows: "Adventists hold different points of view on many issues. The question is Why do we refuse to eat 'unclean meats'? Scripture says that certain foods are ceremonially unclean [Lev. 11:4]. Paul seems to claim that all ceremonial distinctions ended when Christ died on the cross [Col. 2:14]. Jesus declared all foods clean [Mark 7:14; see Rom. 14:14].

"Adventists do not usually eat these foods. The problem is the reason. Is it because they are 'unclean' in themselves, or is it because they are simply unfit for food? Is the law of clean and unclean still binding?

"Let's organize ourselves into groups of three or four and discuss this issue for 10 minutes, and afterward we'll hear from each group." The teacher then leads the class in a general discussion. *Guide the discussion but do not dominate it.*

APPLICATION

The last step in my teaching plan is to choose an activity related to my aim that will assist learners to discover the implications of the truths of the lesson and lead them to commit themselves to action. "Let them [Sabbath school teachers] lay plans to make a practical application of the lesson." [4]

Here are a few suggestions: 1. Keep the pages of the Bible turning. Bible truth will produce right action. 2. Make the Bible contemporary. Use lots of life illustrations. 3. Focus on change. If you know that John has a sub-Christian attitude toward racial issues, you may tactfully include something in your lesson to help him. 4. Lead class members through simulated experiences. "What would you do if you were . . . ?" "How would you apply Matthew 6:24 in this situation?" Create hypothetical examples.

WHAT CAN I PLAN FOR THEM TO DO?

It should be clear by now that your preparation involves planning things for the learner to do more than just what you are going to say. "Involvement" is the key word. When learners actively search Scripture, paraphrase, classify or compare, or resolve conflict or reconcile different points of view, they participate intellectually and emotionally.

SAMPLE TEACHING PLAN:

Central Truth of the lesson: _____

Life Needs of students: _____

Lesson Aim (a very brief statement of a learning goal): _____

Attention Step (use a visual, a story, or a learning activity): _____

Into the Word (choose activities that will give your class a problem to solve or make discoveries that will lead into actual Bible study): _____

Application (select an activity that will lead them to commit themselves to action): _____

LECTURE AND VISUAL AIDS

When did you last hear a lecture? You probably hear one or more every day—a staff meeting, a sales-person at your door, your supervisor on the job, or comments from a parent or spouse. Every Sabbath you hear a sermon. Yes, lecture has its place. It is still the most popular method of teaching in spite of its serious limitations. And it is true that many people prefer the safe haven of anonymity where they can enjoy stimulating ideas without fear of being asked a question. But lecture has some glaring weaknesses. "When the adult teacher is lecturing, the class atmosphere is teacher-centered, teacher-directed, and teacher-dominated. The teacher is at the center of the stage and is actually doing the most learning. Why? Because he is the one most involved in the learning process. People learn most effectively when they are involved and can discuss ideas. And that is exactly what the lecture teacher is not doing. . . . If the lecturer would measure the results of his teaching in terms of changed ideas and lives, perhaps he would begin to revise his appraisal of its effectiveness." [5]

Have you ever noticed how your mind tends to wander during a sermon or a lecture? A lecturer would ordinarily talk at the rate of 125 to 150 words per minute. But the average person thinks from 400 to 800 words per minute. That's the reason our minds want to wander—they get bored. Educators tell us that about 31 percent of the time during a lecture our minds are not on the topic. A great misconception is the notion that "talking is teaching, and listening is learning."

I often use a brief lecture to review a past lesson or to introduce a new unit of curriculum. If I have a large class—more than 50—I tend to depend more on lecture. But I often combine lecture with other methods. A brief lecture can be used with an Agree-Disagree exercise, buzz groups, circle response, creative drawing, or other activity (see chapter 12).

Here are a few guidelines when employing the lecture format: 1. Build upon the present knowledge of the learner. Use simple language and lots of action words. 2. Deal with concepts rather than just factual information. 3. Stimulate the imagination, arouse curiosity, and employ challenging thought questions that grab attention and put the mind in gear. 4. Gather sufficient material to make your lecture interesting. Organize your main ideas and present them in chronological order. 5. Use lots of illustrations to help clarify points and make transitions between the points of the outline. 6. Get involved in your subject and use your voice to enhance your message. Remember, a conversational tone is best.

VISUAL AIDS AND ILLUSTRATIONS
For centuries writers and teachers have recognized the power of visual aids and illustrations. Shakespeare wrote:

"Tongues in trees, books in the running
brooks,
Sermons in stones, and good in every
thing."

Yes, a picture is worth a thousand words. Jesus was a master with illustrations and visuals. At least 61 times in the four Gospels Jesus used illustrations as teaching aids: the figless fig tree, a Roman coin, a child, a net. They were concrete things that He employed to teach abstract truths.

I use lots of visual aids because they grab and hold attention. All I have to do is draw a circle on a chalkboard, for example, and almost everybody immediately looks my way. Try walking into your junior Sabbath school or a sixth-grade Bible class with a big paper sack and place it on your desk, and you will have lots of curiosity. Peel a banana, cut a lemon, or take a saltshaker from your pocket, and everybody watches you.

An orange is a powerful agent in illustrating the church. Made up of segments, it has an outside covering that forms it into a unit, and has a sweet content. Each aspect will help you illustrate the nature of the church. Visual reinforcements continue to make an impact long after the lesson is over.

At the present time I am teaching a large Sabbath school class in a church sanctuary. Although it is inconvenient, I still bring my flip chart every week and use it extensively. Maps and charts are indispensable in teaching the Bible. You enhance learning when you can trace the journeys of Israel or of Paul on a map. And it is impossible to clearly teach the 2300-year prophecy, or the millennium, without using charts.

Education and industry constantly employ overhead projectors. I like an overhead because I can face my audience and reinforce my message with artwork, charts, or outlines. Filmstrips and slides are also valuable and easily obtainable for many topics. Videotapes are having a great impact on education.

But this is work, you say. Yes, it is, but it pays. The truth we are presenting is crucial, and our learners are precious. Let's pay the price, do the work. Then we can ask for the Holy Spirit's blessing.

---

[1] John T. Sisemore, *Blueprint for Teaching* (Nashville: Broadman Press, 1964), p. 45.

[2] White, *Education*, pp. 233, 234.

[3] *Teaching Techniques for the Adult Sabbath School*, p. 41.

[4] White, *Counsels on Sabbath School Work*, pp. 113, 114.

[5] H. Norman Wright, *Ways to Help Them Learn* (Glendale, Calif.: Gospel Light Publications, 1974), pp. 105, 106.

Chapter 11

Discussion and Strategic Questioning

You are sitting in a school cafeteria eating lunch with a group of academy students when Dan says to you, "That discussion in Bible class was really something else! I like your class because it has lots of life, action, and good discussion." Such a comment would make your day, wouldn't it? Discussion is exciting! It stimulates learners as nothing else can do. "Discussion invigorates the mind, opens new worlds of thought. It brings fresh insights from many minds and points of view. . . . Good class discussion, like animated conversation with a friend, is exhilarating and enjoyable. 'Iron sharpeneth iron; so a man sharpeneth the countenance of his friend' (Prov. 27:17)."[1]

So what is discussion? Someone defined it as a "cooperative adventure in search of truth." I like to think of it as the democratic process in action. Our challenge is to direct the discussion and to help learners grapple with "the big ideas" of Bible truth. The lecture method reminds me of golf. The teacher just keeps on hitting the ball. The discussion method resembles tennis more—ideas get batted back and forth. Make the discussion as interesting as possible, and draw the quiet student into the talk in spite of his or her timidity. Some have said that the discussion method is just "group talk" or a "pooling of ignorance." Not so. In reality, good discussion will spark ideas and get the creative juices flowing. It is not a series of dialogues between the teacher and the individual student. Good discussion, directed by the teacher, should take place among the members of the class.

THE VALUE OF DISCUSSION

When you have 25 students together, you have a wide scope of information, insights, and attitudes. I have discovered that group solutions to problems are far superior to those coming from any individual member. And it is interesting to note how discussion can bring two conflicting opinions to a higher view than possible without the encounter. Have you noticed how discussion checks on the thinking processes? Children and adolescents tend to accept the consensus of a group more readily than the pronouncements of an authority figure. Another advantage of discussion is that it helps the learner to listen, to weigh the evidence, and to make sound judgments. And it also enables students to develop skills of self-expression. Fellowship deepens as they share their hopes, fears, and beliefs with one another. Discussion draws students close to one another in Christian community. This principle holds true in family life or in a church board meeting as well as in a formal class setting.

GUIDELINES IN THE USE OF DISCUSSION

It is important to keep the spotlight on the Word of God. This helps to avoid aimless talk. Keep the pages of the Bible turning. If we listen to God's idea first and then share our thoughts and feelings, we are more apt to "rightly divide the word of truth." It's interesting to note how Jesus often planned for discussion. He was always asking questions. "What think ye?" was a favorite expression. The four Gospels record Him raising more than 100 questions. Your role is that of a leader, a stimulator, a guide, an enabler, and a resource person. I have heard teachers announce that they welcome discussion, but it was obvious that they were so bent on telling about their own discoveries that they crowded student involvement out. In essence, they were saying, "Don't interrupt me."

As a teacher I should be an authority on the content of the lesson, but I should never be authoritarian in attitude. That will squelch discussion as nothing else. The autocratic or authoritarian teacher makes up his or her mind before class on all the questions. Obviously, it does not mean that teachers should not share their ideas. We have convictions and should defend them. But let us first wait until the students have expressed their thoughts. However, I must never abdicate my role as leader. It is important to keep the discussion on track. "Perhaps we have spent enough time on this aspect. Let's consider . . ." Sometimes I have had to interrupt a lively discussion and move the group forward to a further idea. Often I will fluctuate from a directive to a nondirective stance as a discussion leader.

CLARIFYING STUDENT RESPONSES

I will ask a student, "Tom, do I hear you saying that . . . ?" Then I paraphrase what I heard him say. Or I may ask him to restate his comment. And as Tom restates his point he will reevaluate and often soften or alter his ideas. Always I must be very careful never to convey rejection. I try to help my learners to focus and sharpen their thinking. John Sisemore says: "Most learners have difficulty clarifying their thinking unless they are able to 'vocalize their confusion' and state their concepts."[2]

The way I handle negative comments or wrong answers has much to do with the emotional climate of my class. When my students recognize that I truly welcome open free discussion and that no one will ever get put down, they are much more apt to participate. *Make your Sabbath school class, Bible class, or family worship a safe place to be.*

Behavior description is another aid you may find helpful in encouraging discussion: "June looks like she disagrees." Or "George and Robert have supplied us with the most input. Who else has a comment?" Sometimes I feel it necessary to project my own feelings: "That idea makes me rather uncomfortable." "I enjoy your sense of humor, George." Feedback is vital in leading a good discussion. The effective teacher will "keep his antenna up" to receive all the signals possible from his or her learners. Study facial expression, posture, and tone of voice to know where your learners are.

Grade school children have their own set of challenges. They love to discuss but tend to all talk at the same time. In their immaturity they do not listen to one another. You might say, "In this class we discuss by raising our hands. When you demonstrate that you can listen while others are talking, we will change the rule." This makes it possible for the teacher to keep the discussion on track and avoid the bedlam of everyone talking at once. Keep challenging them to listen to one another and thus earn the right to comment.

THE ART OF QUESTIONING
The right question is the key to good discussion.

Perhaps you recall Francis Bacon's famous statement that a skillful question is half the answer. The quality of your questions will greatly influence your effectiveness as a Bible teacher. I use questions because they attract attention, break the ice, and get the discussion under way. Questions tell how much knowledge my learners have and get them to participate and share the spotlight. Also, questions provide a useful way of reviewing the lesson and of helping learners to struggle with problems. I spend considerable time planning my questions and incorporating them into my teaching plan.

The interaction between the instructor and the learner is very complex and usually rapid. Most of us do not know ahead of time exactly what questions we will introduce at a given moment. Ronald Hyman says that "the ability at a given juncture in the lesson to ask an appropriate question, one which will continue the forward thrust of the interaction, requires a framework." [3] It is here that the teacher's strategy of questioning comes into play. By strategy he means *"a carefully prepared plan involving a sequence of steps designed to achieve a given goal."* [4]

Hyman suggests mixing the type or format of questions. "Teachers generally ask the same type of question without achieving a recognizable mixture. Thus, one type of question predominates." [5] Teachers—especially beginning teachers—tend to concentrate on factual questions. One researcher found that "about 60 percent of teachers' questions require students to recall facts . . . !" [6]

Have you ever observed a teacher play the "Guess what I'm thinking" game? He asks a question, the student responds, and the teacher says, "No, that's not what I had in mind." He may turn to another student and repeat the same question. I've seen teachers go from student to student until someone guesses precisely what the teacher had in mind. What does this accomplish? It communicates to the student that it is not as important to think as it is to give the exact answer the teacher had in mind. I have heard more tactful teachers say, "George, that was a good try and that's helpful. Does anyone else have an idea?" At this point I myself may rephrase the question. It is more important, in my opinion, to encourage thoughtful analysis than just to get the student to come up with exactly the right words.

Once I observed a teacher fire a question at a student who was disrupting the class. The adult used the question as a disciplinary measure. It seems to me that the teacher who employs questions as a method for securing order is saying in effect, "If you don't behave or pay attention, I'll attack you with a question, and if you don't know the right answer, you will obviously be embarrassed." I feel uncomfortable with that way of securing order. The problem is that it doesn't encourage creative thinking. A student who feels intimidated by a question is not in a frame of mind to be very creative. Moreover, it seems a bit duplicitous for the teacher to pretend that he or she wants the learner to thoughtfully participate when his or her real concern is with control.

Consider some different kinds of questions. Literal questions are simple questions that the majority of the students are able to answer. We may use such words as who, what, when, how, where. Such questions deal with the cognitive domain. Interpretive questions are more difficult. Demanding reasoning from cause to effect, they begin with why, what reason, what caused, or please explain.

In talking about the purpose of teacher questions, Hyman says, "No other single pedagogical technique yields so much return for your effort."[7] Catherine Landreth said that the words "'Ask, don't tell' might

profitably be engraved, at teacher eye level, on the wall
of every nursery school and kindergarten. . . . A question involves a child or a person of any age in a way that
a statement does not."[8]

TOLERANCE FOR SILENCE

We talked earlier about a common problem of parents, preachers, and teachers—their poor listening
skills. (Most of us have the mistaken notion that others
expect us to talk.) And why is it we feel so awkward
during moments of silence? It's probably from the mistaken idea that "talking is teaching, and listening is
learning." All of us need to develop a "tolerance for silence." The ability to remain silent is one of the most effective tools in communication. So ask a good question
and then wait for an answer. Give learners time to col-
lect their thoughts. It is too easy to rush in and answer
our own question. Ask the question, keep eye contact,
and wait. Should the learners squirm a bit, it means
they're thinking. If you do not break the silence, pretty
soon someone will venture to respond. "Tom, you look
like you are on the verge of a comment. Do you have
something to share?"

We talked earlier about "selective listening" and
"monitoring conversation." Too often I find myself listening just enough to refute what someone else is saying. At
other times I seem to be formulating my responses instead
of sincerely trying to understand what my students are
really telling me. I say again that genuine, supportive listening demands the graces of the Spirit—patience, tolerance, and Christian love. Parents, pastors, and teachers
who master the skill of listening with the heart will find an
inside track to the minds and affections of their learners.

One survey of teens raised the question "What is

your greatest gripe against your parents?" By far the largest response was "My dad and mom will not listen to me." I have tried for years to develop this skill, but I certainly have not arrived. However, I am sure that Jesus was a good listener. Let's try to develop this skill. It will enhance discussion, demonstrate that we care about persons, and encourage spiritual growth.

---

[1] Betz, *Teaching Techniques for the Adult Sabbath School*, p. 73.

[2] Sisemore, *Blueprint for Teaching*, p. 28.

[3] Ronald T. Hyman, *Strategic Questioning* (Englewood Cliffs, N.J.: Prentice-Hall, Inc., 1979), pp. xi, xii.

[4] *Ibid.*, p. xiii.

[5] *Ibid.*, p. 33.

[6] Meredith D. Gall, "The Use of Questions in Teaching," *Review of Educational Research* 40, No. 5 (December 1970): 713.

[7] Hyman, p. 5.

[8] Catherine Landreth, *Preschool Learning and Teaching* (New York: Harper and Row, 1972), pp. 12, 11.

Chapter 12

Bible Learning Activities

"What I hear I forget;
What I see I remember;
What I do I learn." [1]

Children remember: 10 percent of what they read,
20 percent of what they hear,
30 percent of what they see,
50 percent of what they hear and see,
70 percent of what they say,
90 percent of what they say and do
(based on research by the University of Texas).[2]
When students interact with what is to be learned and become actively involved in the subject, their retention greatly improves, a fact portrayed in what one can call the "Triangle of Learning." [3]

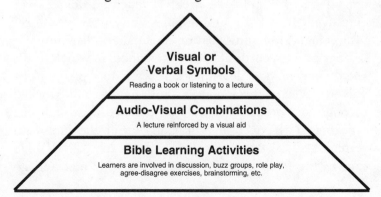

**Visual or
Verbal Symbols**
Reading a book or listening to a lecture

Audio-Visual Combinations
A lecture reinforced by a visual aid

Bible Learning Activities
Learners are involved in discussion, buzz groups, role play,
agree-disagree exercises, brainstorming, etc.

Obviously, the lower you go on the triangle, the more efficient the learning. The visual and verbal symbols at the top of the triangle are the least efficient. When students read a book or listen to the teacher, they will have a comparatively low retention factor. Verbal symbols are the most abstract of all teaching devices.

As we go down the triangle we see that the audiovisual combinations increase learning value—this is why professional teachers use such things as chalkboards, flip charts, overheads, and teaching pictures. It is at the bottom of the triangle that the most efficient learning occurs—the direct learning experience. Here the pupil learns by *doing* rather than by just listening or seeing. Bible teachers who lead their classes to identify, choose, evaluate, contrast, or compare are instructing near the bottom of the triangle. Drawing, writing, role plays, field trips—any kind of direct participation has excellent retention value. But we should employ all the strategies indicated on the triangle. When one teaches from the top of the triangle to the bottom, it incorporates all factors. Our challenge is to keep the learner *involved!*

Jesus, the greatest teacher the world has ever known, demonstrated some outstanding instructional methods. Take the sacrificial system as an example. I consider it probably the greatest teaching device ever employed. It calls for emotional involvement, visual reinforcement, touching, tasting, feeling, and listening.

Scripture records at least 50 instances in which Jesus used some kind of learning activity. Most of them involved at least three senses, and nearly half worked through four or more senses. For instance, Jesus told the servants at the wedding of Cana, "Fill the jars with water. . . . Now draw some out" (John 2:7, 8, NIV). He said to the lame man, "Get up, take your mat and go home" (Mark 2:11, NIV). One day after a sermon Jesus said to the disciples, "Put out into deep water, and let down the nets for a catch" (Luke 5:4, NIV). Every miracle was an activity and a visual reinforcement.

Wanting us to remember His sacrifice in our behalf, Jesus gave us something to do. "For whenever you eat this bread and drink this cup, you proclaim the Lord's death until he comes" (1 Cor. 11:26, NIV). At the Communion service we see, hear, touch, and taste, and powerful learning occurs. Such direct experiences reach our consciousness and become indelibly impressed upon us. Baptism is another learning activity Jesus gave us. In it God's people act out a profound truth. "What a blessing it would be if all would teach as Jesus taught!"[4]

GUIDELINES FOR CHOOSING
AND USING BIBLE LEARNING ACTIVITIES

Every teacher faces the question "What method should I use for this class?" Let's consider some guidelines: 1. A learning activity should fit the lesson content. Some topics lend themselves to writing, others to discussion groups, or brief lectures. 2. Bible learning activities must work within the learners' cognitive development, age, sex, and environment. 3. How much time will this activity take? Do we have the equipment? 4. The current Bible knowledge of the learners and your aim will influence your choice. 5. Don't overuse a good activity. Use the element of surprise.

Some of the following activities will help you reach your cognitive aim. Others will aid your affective or attitudinal goals. Still others will assist in reaching your behavioral objectives and transferring theory to life. Many of the activities suggested are exercises that will provide learners with practice in selecting the best and rejecting the worst elements in our society. Values clarification exercises will enable older children and youth to build their own value system.

Our objective is to help young people think through their values and make right choices. The Valuegenesis report indicates that we need more thought-provoking activities in our churches and schools. Only 31 percent of the students in grades 9-12 and 36 percent in grades 6-8 feel that our religious education programs are of high quality. Only 23 percent of the learners in grades 9-12 and 44 percent of students in grades 6-8 consider their congregational programs thought-provoking.[5] We want our young people to examine their beliefs and to compare them with the Word of God.

Always select exercises that will provide practice in reasoning, thinking, and choosing. Children are more apt to alter their behavior after they have had opportunity to think things through and share with their peers. Here are 31 activities commonly used in Bible classes:

1. Comparing
2. Memorizing
3. Observing
4. Classifying
5. Interpreting
6. Criticizing
7. Look for assumptions
8. Imagining
9. Collecting and organizing data
10. Hypothesizing
11. Creating modern-day parables
12. Open-ended sentences
13. Multiple choice
14. Interview and forum
15. Research report and forum
16. Brainstorming
17. Buzz groups
18. Neighbor nudging
19. Circle response
20. Chain reaction
21. Case study
22. Paraphrasing
23. Role playing
24. Pantomime
25. Charades
26. Psychodrama
27. Creative drawing
28. Listening teams
29. Agree/Disagree exercise
30. Film talk-back: "What would you do?"
31. "How would your life be different if you were to put this truth into practice?"

The following activities are graded, but in some cases you can modify and use them on a different level.

EARLY CHILDHOOD AND CHILDHOOD

The purpose of these activities is to help young children learn Bible truths by providing a variety of interesting activities. Bible learning centers are important (i.e., art, music, blocks, home living centers, books, puzzles, nature, audio, etc.). The Bible should have a central place as far as possible in every activity. I like to see an open Bible on the table as a centerpiece. It helps create an ambience of reverence and respect. (Reverence does not always mean that children should be quiet and fold their hands.) In telling a story or in a Bible learning activity, call attention to the words of the Bible and point to them as you open the Bible. Remember that young children need sensory experiences to learn about God and nature. They must see, touch, feel, smell, and handle. Consider their interest and attention span.

PICTURES

1. Select a simple verse from the Bible containing one idea. Choose two or three pictures with one of them reinforcing the message of the Bible and ask the children to point to the picture that best represents the verse. Do the same with a story or a song. 2. Select pictures of desirable and undesirable conduct and invite the children to pick those showing good conduct. 3. Using three or four pictures, ask the children to pretend they are people in the picture by standing or sitting as those in the picture are doing. 4. Ask a child to tell a story suggested by a picture. 5. Help the children to "make up" a story about a nature picture.

BLOCK BUILDERS

Educators usually consider blocks the backbone of any educational program for small children. Blocks help them to develop coordination, recognize basic shapes, and provide a medium to create what they see and understand. Encourage each child to build for himself or herself. Sitting on the floor, tell the story of how God took down the walls of Jericho. Allow the children to build the Jericho wall and knock it down. A little imagination will suggest many ways that you can use blocks in teaching the Bible. As you do so, open your Bible and point to the story. Our aim is to help children see the Bible as a book of activity and fun.

Also allow children to play by themselves.

GAMES

Select tiny bits of food that are sweet, bitter, sour, or salty. Talk about our tongues and how God made us so we can taste many good things. Ask them to tell you what their favorite food is.

As a guessing game, ask children to feel an item in a paper sack: a comb, a pencil, a piece of sandpaper, a rock, a pinecone, a leaf, etc. Let them identify the items by touch. Talk about how God placed little "wires" in our bodies to send messages to our brains to tell us what we see and feel. Discuss God's gift of touch.[6]

DRAWING

Say to the children, "You may draw a picture of something nice you could do for someone at home, school, or church. Draw a picture of something that makes you happy.

"Next, draw a picture of something that you need or want." Then talk to them about how God supplies these things for us.

NATURE ACTIVITIES

A nature walk can be a thrilling experience. Ahead of time look for a cobweb, a bird's nest, some interesting leaves, or a specific kind of tree. You could use a walking rope to keep the children together. Take containers for specimens that you find along the way. Stop for a close look at insects, rocks, or flowers. Talk about the wonderful things that God has made. Be sure to allow the children to touch and handle things as far as possible. Answer their questions. A magnifying glass is a wonderful help.

Indoor gardens are good teaching devices. Avocado seeds and sweet potatoes grow quickly and provide lots of excitement. Again, a magnifying glass is an important accessory for any nature activity. Plant seeds so the children can see them germinate. "Sprinkle grass seed, lettuce, or radish seeds on a damp sponge. Place the sponge in a shallow container and keep it moist. . . . A corncob soaked in water and sprinkled with grass seed makes an interesting planter."[7] Magnets can also serve as wonderful teachers.

Make a vegetable person. Gather the children around a pumpkin, cut it open, and talk about the color and the consistency of the material inside. How does it feel? How does it smell? Make holes in the pumpkin for the nose, eyes, and mouth of the head. Let the children feel the seeds. Show them what holds the seeds together.[8]

WATER

Water activities provide lots of thrills for small children. Such things as bubble soap, paper cups, and drinking straws make water play interesting to them.

Most children enjoy blowing bubbles. Soak two identical cloths in water, hang one in the sunshine and one in the shade and see which drys first, then talk about it. Ice is another good teaching medium. Discuss what makes things float and what causes them to sink.

Many activities involve sight: a kaleidoscope, a prism, tempera paints in primary colors. All these can teach us about God. "Can you think of something that God made that is green?" Place a prism in the sunlight and look at the colors in the rainbow as it refracts the light. Help the children name the colors.

ACTIVITIES TO ACCOMPANY STORIES

(These exercises are for children in the lower grades.)

Tell a Bible story centered on Joseph, Esther, Daniel, etc. Print the names of the chief characters on the board and ask the children to select their favorite. Ask them to write or tell three things that they like best about the character they picked. Let them choose the one that they would want most to be like and tell why.

Talk about the coming of Jesus and what we should do to get ready. Have the children list, tell, or draw five things that they want most to take with them to heaven. Ask them to tell two things to do to get ready to go to heaven with Jesus.

IMAGINING

1. You are in heaven and about to try out your new wings. Write a paragraph or tell what you would do.

2. What would it be like to be a snowflake? Write a paragraph or tell how you think it would feel.

3. You are visiting another planet and suddenly you see Jesus. What would you do? Write a paragraph or tell about it.

4. Begin a story and ask a child to finish it using his or her imagination.

MIDDLE CHILDHOOD
(middle and upper grades)

MEMORIZING FUN

Print a memory verse on the chalkboard, preferably a longer or more difficult one to learn. Ask the children to read it with you in unison and then briefly talk about the meaning. Be *sure* that every child knows the meaning of every word. (Ask for definitions.) Then read the verse in unison three or four more times. Erase four or five words and then ask the children to read the verse again, filling in the missing words. Repeat this process until the children can repeat the verse entirely from memory. Review the verse later in the day. You will be amazed at how rapidly they learn.

COMPARING

After a Bible lesson or story involving three or four characters or interesting events, ask the children to write or explain the differences between them. For example: Jacob and Esau; Abraham and Lot; Peter and Judas; Noah's ark and Peter's boat; a mother's work and a father's work; the earth before the Flood and after the Flood; etc.

HYPOTHESIZING

The purpose of these exercises is to help the children to use their imagination.

What would happen if (1) Jesus had not been born; (2) we could not pray; (3) someone took the Bible away from everybody; (4) the law of the land said we must attend church on Sunday; (5) your church had no pastor; (6) the church burned down? Ask the children either to write a paragraph or to discuss their reactions.

DRAWING OR CONSTRUCTING

Following a Bible lesson or a story, give the children 10 minutes to work on a mural. Let them select some part of the story that impresses them. Provide paper and colored pencils or pens. Have them, for example: (1) draw persons displaying certain characteristics such as pride, humility, envy, happiness; (2) draw a picture of something nice they could do for their mothers this evening; (3) draw a picture of Jesus teaching the people on the mountainside near the Sea of Galilee; (4) create a mobile out of a Bible verse by printing the words on construction paper.

INTERVIEW AN AUTHORITY FIGURE

Announce to your class that you are going to invite an authority figure for them to interview. It could be a firefighter, a nurse, a physician, a minister, a carpenter, etc. Have the class write questions to ask. Form groups to choose at least five questions to present. Appoint a group leader and secretary for each group. Tell them that you will review the questions before the visitor arrives.

MATCHING

Following a Bible story or a lesson, write a paragraph describing three or four everyday predicaments. Place your learners in groups and ask them to select from the lesson some solutions to the problems. Have them explain why they think the solutions will help.

Make a list of animals, birds, insects, or other things in nature that illustrate a human characteristic such as gentleness, caring, neatness, nurture, cruelty, craftiness, slyness, selfishness, diligence, power, curiosity, pride, show-offishness, loyalty, friendliness, gracefulness, etc. Match the insect, bird, etc., to a human characteristic. Many examples appear in the Bible.

I LEARNED STATEMENTS

This provides an opportunity to clarify and reinforce what they have learned from a story or lesson. On the chalkboard the teacher writes: I LEARNED THAT . . . ; I REALIZED THAT . . . ; I NOTICED THAT . . . ; I DISCOVERED THAT . . . ; I WAS SURPRISED THAT . . . ; I WAS PLEASED THAT . . . ; I WAS DISPLEASED THAT . . . ; WHAT IF . . . ? Then ask the children to think back over the lesson or story and write a paragraph (or tell something) beginning with the above statements.

BRAINSTORMING

The teacher writes a problem on the chalkboard. Example: "How can we improve race relations in our school?" Tell the students you want rapid-fire, spontaneous suggestions. Write their responses on the board but do not criticize or evaluate the ideas. The teacher stimulates and encourages but does not give answers or suggestions. After a few minutes, go back over the written list of ideas, combining and grouping them, and then discuss how the school might actually implement their suggestions.

BUZZ GROUPS

(This you could possibly use with sixth graders.) A buzz group is a small group of three to six persons. The purpose is to involve every member in discussing a relevant question. Appoint a moderator and recorder for each group. Then ask for a two-minute report from each group.

CIRCLE RESPONSE

The teacher asks an opinion question and gives each person an opportunity to respond. Go around the room and involve as many learners as possible.

BIBLE PARAPHRASE

Ask sixth graders to rewrite a Bible passage in their own words. First talk about the meaning of the verse, then ask them to put it in their own words. Afterward have various learners read their paraphrase. Then you may read the passage from some modern speech translation. Be sure to summarize and lead the class to the application.

AGREE/DISAGREE

Prepare a series of opinion statements based on a story or lesson. Ask the students to number from 1 to 10 and write the word "Agree" or "Disagree" for each statement that you are about to read. Grade the statements according to the cognitive ability of the students.

FILM TALK-BACK

After showing a film, filmstrip, or video, the teacher directs thought questions to the class. Encourage the group to make notes during the film in order to discuss it more intelligently.

WHAT WOULD YOU DO?

The teacher poses a life situation problem. It should be realistic, practical, and appropriate to the grade level of the class. Write the problem on the chalkboard—such as "What would you do if you were taking an evening walk and suddenly . . . ?" You could divide the class into groups of three to five and ask them to discuss the issue for five minutes. Then do a circle response.

YOUTH

These exercises will help your students clarify values. I have rephrased and adapted the following nine activities for Bible class.[9]

VOTE YOUR VALUES

This exercise provides an opportunity to make an affirmation on a variety of issues. Ask students to point their thumbs UP for an affirmation and DOWN if they disagree.

How many of you (1) think that God is too strict? (2) that Sabbath school is exciting? (3) that school should have fewer rules? etc. Make up your own statements based on your lesson.

THINGS YOU ENJOY

Here you will seek to help youth build a good life and at the same time have them consider the call of discipleship. Ask them to list on a page the things that they love to do. After they have completed their list, lead them to consider each thing in terms of what Christ would have them do. Have them put a checkmark by those they feel are OK, a question mark by those they are undecided on, and an X by those that are definitely out of harmony with God's revealed will.

RANK ORDER

Write a list of values on the chalkboard and ask your students to rank them in the order of their importance. Example: "Place the following in the order of their importance: (1) having fun every day; (2) evaluating your performance; (3) prayer; (4) careful planning; (5) a good mixture of work and play; (6) the searching of God's Word; (7) care in selecting friends, etc."

CARVE YOUR PIE

Draw a large circle on the chalkboard. Divide it into four sections. Explain: "This circle represents a part of your life. Consider how you use a typical day. Each slice represents six hours. Now think about how many hours you spend each day in the following areas of a typical school day.

1. Sleep
2. School
3. Work and chores
4. With friends
5. Homework
6. Prayer and Bible study
7. Family, including meals
8. Watching television

"Consider the following questions:

"1. Are you satisfied with the relative sizes of the slices?

"2. How much time does Jesus get?

"3. Should you change some of your priorities?"

YOUR COAT OF ARMS

Here we want youth to examine their lives and consider their values. Draw a coat of arms on the board and divide into quadrants.

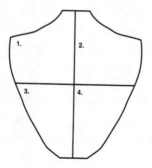

Ask the students to draw a symbol or picture in the appropriate area on the coat of arms in response to the numbered statements below:

1. Quadrant No. 1: My family "roots."
2. Quadrant No. 2: What Jesus means to me.
3. Quadrant No. 3: My motto that I try to live by.
4. Quadrant No. 4: My goal for this life.

You could use this in the ninth- or tenth-grade Bible class when the students are studying the book of Matthew. Begin by reading Matthew 1 (genealogy). Then talk about family backgrounds: nationality, family origin, life goals, etc. Allow them to work about 20 minutes in class, then have them take the coat of arms home and work on it. Encourage them to be artistic by using marking pencils or pens.

YOUR CLOTHES TELL ABOUT YOU

Our clothes say a lot about us. However, it is a particularly sensitive subject with teenagers. The purpose of this exercise is to help young people look at their clothing and ask themselves, "What does my clothing say about me?"

Item of clothing	What I want my clothing to say about me	What my clothing does in fact say to others about me
1. Shirt/blouse		
2. Slacks, skirt, jeans		
3. Shoes		
4. Sweater, jacket		
5. Watch or other items worn		

Such an exercise provides a marvelous opportunity for young people to examine their clothing and to make decisions about the kind of statements they want their clothing to make about them. Organize into discussion groups.

YOUR LIFE

(This exercise confronts the student with the reality of life and death.)

Ask learners to draw a horizontal line across their papers with a short vertical line at each end. "On the left side write the date of your birth. On the right side write the date you think you might die (if Jesus doesn't come first). Write your age. Place a mark where you are right now between your birth and death. Write today's date under this mark."

Have them write their obituary by finishing the following open-ended sentence: "When I die I want people to remember me as . . ."

Help the youth to see that we live this life only once. Tell them they can ask Jesus to enable them to live in a way that they will be proud to look back on.

MAKE A CONTRACT WITH YOURSELF

Young people struggle with bad habits and practices. Encourage your students to make a contract with themselves about some change that they would like to make. They should consider starting something they should do or stopping something they don't believe they should do.

Persuade them to be realistic and to give careful thought and prayer to their contract.

VALUES PLACEMENT

The purpose of this exercise is to help young people look at issues and to decide what they believe about them. It will lead them to discover that life is not all black and white.

First the teacher draws a long line on the chalkboard, then the class members discuss their positions on various topics. For example:

"Suppose you are a parent of a 16-year-old boy/girl. On the left side of this line write 'COMPLETE SOCIAL FREEDOM' and on the opposite side 'STRICT CONTROL OF HOURS, RECREATION, COMPANY, ETC.'

"Where do you feel is your position on this continuum or line? Do you think a boy or girl of 16 should come and go as he/she pleases? With whomever he/she pleases? Or would you opt for the absolute control indicated on the right side of the continuum? Take 10 minutes now to think this through and place yourself somewhere along the horizonal line." (Then use their responses as a basis for discussion.)

ROLE PLAY

Organize your students into groups of six to feature a role play depicting the topic of the day's Bible lesson. Allow them 15 minutes to plan their role plays. Following each role play, the class decides the lesson they can learn from the skit.

HIERARCHY OF PHYSICAL LOVE
(for academy juniors or seniors)

The teacher talks about the physical aspects of human love. On the chalkboard he or she indicates the steps to the ultimate expression of love in sexual intercourse:

1. A look and a smile
2. A touch of the fingertips
3. Hand-holding
4. A gentle kiss
5. A deep kiss
6. The handling of genitals
7. Sexual intercourse

Then the teacher asks the class: "Where would you

draw the line? What is appropriate for a Christian young person 17 or 18 years of age? What does the Bible teach?" A very straightforward discussion follows dealing with the principles of Christian courtship. (The test here is honesty and reality.)

PREPARING FOR SEMESTER EXAMINATIONS

The class divides into groups of five or six and the teacher provides a long list of questions from which he or she will select the final semester examination. Using Bibles, textbooks, and workbooks, each group looks for the right answers. The group appoints a secretary to speak for them and record the number of correct answers. The teacher asks the questions and provides right answers, rotating from group to group. The team with the most correct answers wins.

ART
(grade school or preschool)

Art provides a marvelous outlet for feelings—positive or negative. Painting and drawing have healing power for troubled children. They are able to create their own world, secure and warm and stable. Drawing or painting gives every child an opportunity to explore and experiment.

Play-Doh is another excellent medium for preschool, kindergarten, and the lower grades. "As I tell the story today, make something about the lesson, and then afterward you may tell us about it if you like." Obviously parents and teachers must allow full liberty for them to create. We are not talking about a professional art class. Allow children to express themselves freely, and teach them about God along the way.

MUSIC AND STORIES

Looking back to my church school days—after 60 years—a few things stand out. One of them is singing at worshiptime. It was a happy time, and I still remember the songs we learned: "Little Feet, Be Careful," "The B-I-B-L-E," "Brighten the Corner Where You Are." Why do I remember those songs? Because it was a joyful time. And the message still echoes in my heart. "Let's talk about the song we just sang. How can you 'brighten the corner where you are'? What does the word 'corner' mean?"

This is an important part of Christian education. Music is a powerful instrument for good or evil. It allows the shy child self-expression, calms the tense and nervous child, and enables the overactive to release stress. Have you ever noticed how children at play make up their own little songs? Rhythm and music seem to be built into their very bones. A God-given outlet for human creativity, it provides marvelous ways to praise God.

PUPPETS

An academy Bible teacher announced: "Tomorrow we are going to put on two puppet shows to illustrate the word 'forgiveness.' We're going to video your productions, and later we will show them to the seventh grade. If you will form into groups, we can plan your productions. You can make your puppets out of paper sacks using bright-colored marking pens." The next day I observed the following: two teenage girls got down behind the teacher's desk and a boy read the script. The script was well written and used two voice registers. The girls did a clever job creating the puppets and acted their parts well. Afterward the teacher led the class in a discussion. The interaction was excellent. I am sure those teens internalized the principle of forgiveness. They may forget the factual information, but they will always feel the importance of forgiveness and recall the fun of their involvement. Puppets used with care and discretion can be powerful tools. Animal mitts work effectively with young children. Drama is a legitimate method of teaching. Use puppets in good taste and avoid the boisterous, the absurd, the ugly, and the grotesque.

The purpose of all activities is to present the gospel on the level of the children and youth in a way that will catch their interest—yes, even fascinate them. It is possible! Employ activities that will touch their muscles, stimulate their minds, and lead them to Jesus.[10]

---

[1] Chinese proverb.

[2] See Betz, *Teaching Techniques*, p. 60.

[3] *Ibid.*

[4] White, *Counsels on Sabbath School Work*, p. 182.

[5] *Valuegenesis Report I*, pp. 29, 30.

[6] See Dolores Rowen, *Ways to Help Them Learn* (Glendale, Calif.: International Center for Learning, 1972), p. 105.

[7] *Ibid.*, pp. 100, 101.

[8] *Ibid.*, pp. 104-108.

[9] See Sidney B. Simon, Leland W. Howe, and Howard Kirschenbaum, *Values Clarification* (New York: Hart Publishing Company, Inc., 1972), pp. 30, 38, 58, 116, 225, 278, 304, 319, 331.

[10] The Bible learning activities in this chapter were drawn from years of practice, observation, and reading. It is impossible to give credit as I would like to.

Chapter 13

Jesus' Teaching Strategies

Have you heard this definition of a college: a teacher at one end of a log and a pupil on the other? Even though the "log" college is famous in Princeton University history, the college on a log today would be an example of reductio ad absurdum. Yet, think about it. The essentials are in place: the teacher, the pupil, and a learning environment (the log). We boast of our sophistication—imposing buildings, beautiful campuses, large comfortable classrooms, libraries, laboratories, computers, and the very latest and best in equipment. But some of the world's most decisive teaching moments have consisted of only a teacher and a pupil. Let us look at Jesus, the Master Teacher, and some great teaching-learning events in His human life on earth.

Jesus was sitting alone at Jacob's well. You remember the story. It was about noon, and He was hot, tired, and thirsty. The disciples had gone to town to buy food. Suddenly a young Samaritan woman appeared with a water jug to draw water. Jesus, always ready to teach, took advantage of the opportunity. How was He to get through to this needy person? It wasn't a generation gap—it was much worse, having not only a social barrier but also a wall of prejudice and sin. But love had a "wit to win." The first duty of a teacher is to get through the walls, whether they be social or age level, and win the confidence of the learner.

Notice Jesus' teaching strategy. I imagine He gave her a big smile and said something like this: "It sure is hot, isn't it! Do you suppose I could have a drink of water?" The Teacher takes the initiative. Love begets trust. And love and trust are the very foundations of learning. Did Jesus teach by objectives? Certainly. He came "to seek and to save that which was lost" (Luke 19:10). Here's a poor woman—mistrusted, looked down upon, and deep in the quagmire of sin—but a candidate for the kingdom. Yes, even the most careless, incorrigible teenage boy in your classroom is not hopeless. He too is a potential candidate for heaven. In fact, he may be nearer and more ready for the gospel than some who appear more promising. We have already referred to the famous principle that learners tend to rise to the expectation of their teachers. Jesus was looking for the key to this woman's heart.[1] I believe that a similar key exists to almost every heart. And love will find the way to it.

Attention is the first law of learning. Jesus got her attention by His odd request, and she was ready to listen. Having earned the right to teach, He moved to the next step in His teaching plan. "If you knew the gift of God and who it is that asks you for a drink, you would have asked him and he would have given you living water" (John 4:10, NIV). Now she was really curious, perhaps a little amused. I rather imagine she sat down, wide-eyed, and just stared at Him. "Living water— what in the world is that? Yes, I'd like that so I won't get thirsty and have to keep coming here to draw water." The teachable moment had arrived. Gently and lovingly He said, "Go, call your husband and come back" (verse 16, NIV). Sometimes pain helps learning. Jesus had touched a sore spot, so she digressed by discussing theology, but He allowed the learner to talk. It is important for learners to articulate their thoughts and feelings. Then Jesus again took the lead in the discussion. He talked about true worship. "God is spirit, and his worshipers must worship in spirit and in truth" (verse 24, NIV). The woman suddenly grasped an entirely new concept of spiritual truth. Gradually it began to dawn on her who her teacher really was. When she refered to the Messiah, Jesus said, "I who speak to you am he" (verse 26, NIV). Amazingly, Jesus had veiled His identity before the doubting, quibbling religious leaders, but He disclosed Himself as the Saviour of the world to a despised outcast of society.

Thrilled and excited, she must have said to herself, "This is too good to keep. I must tell my friends." She forgot to give Jesus the drink He asked for, forgot her water pot, and took off on a run to town. I am sure Jesus must have smiled and felt a deep sense of satisfaction. This is the teacher's reward. The learner has learned, and transfer has occurred. How do I know? She became a missionary. "Many of the Samaritans from that town believed in him because of the woman's testimony" (verse 39, NIV).

Let's look at some of the important elements in this teaching-learning encounter: 1. Jesus taught from an objective (Luke 19:10). 2. Jesus saw in the learner great potential. 3. He truly cared for His student. 4. He studied the learner—that is, He knew all about her. 5. He got her attention and used visual aids—water, a drink, the fountain. 6. He used the familiar to interpret the unfamiliar. 7. He was a good listener. 8. He showed respect for her and increased her self-worth. 9. He taught in a way that would meet her felt needs. 10. He created and recognized the teachable moment.

JESUS TEACHES NICODEMUS

Jesus was enjoying a few moments of quiet on the Mount of Olives one lovely evening when suddenly a distinguished-looking Pharisee came to Him. Courteous and complimentary, the religious leader called Jesus "Rabbi." Again, we have Him with a single learner. His objective was salvation (Luke 19:10). Jesus saw great potential in this sophisticated Pharisee. I'm sure He communicated love and acceptance. The Teacher recognized the learner's need. As with the woman at the well, He employed dialogue and discussion. To get his attention, He used the unexpected. Nicodemus wanted to talk theology, but Jesus avoided his esoteric approach and moved to the practical. "I tell you the truth, no one can see the kingdom of God unless he is born again" (John 3:3, NIV). Nicodemus' great desire was to secure inclusion in that kingdom. Jesus told him how it can be done.

Our Saviour's use of metaphors here is unique. He talked about birth, water, Spirit, wind, Light, darkness, and a serpent. Again, the great Teacher moved from the known to the unknown. "In Christ's teaching the unknown was illustrated by the known; divine truths by earthly things with which the people were most familiar."[2]

Jesus used parables extensively and was a great storyteller. Many of His stories contained an element of mystery, thus creating the possibility of later discussion by the people. I can hear them saying, for example, "Just who is the 'elder brother'?" This led to discovery learning. "No more effective method of instruction could He have employed."[3] His selection of stories had great variety in order to appeal to different hearers. If we wish to teach as Jesus did, we will be constantly on the lookout for stories and illustrations — especially in nature.

Here we have an example of the Teacher adapting His methods to the specific learner. Nicodemus was a highly cultured, well-educated man. Jesus met him on his own ground, but He simplified profound truth by the use of metaphor. Jesus and Nicodemus were wrestling with a "big idea" — the kingdom of God. As one educator said, "Real thinking begins with a problem." But more than anything else, it was Jesus' moral earnestness, His love, and His tact that won the respect of the Jewish intellectual. Jesus sowed the seed, and after three years it bore fruit. Nicodemus became a humble, faithful follower of Jesus of Nazareth.

In our teaching, let us reflect that of Jesus as much as possible.

JESUS AND CHILDREN

Child abuse has become a national disgrace! Any hospital emergency room physician will tell you about little children brought in with wounds and broken bones from beatings, torture, and sexual abuse. Incest is common. In our large cities adults still force thousands of children to labor long hours.

Thankfully most church members are not guilty of such heinous sins against children, but what about indifference? Like the furniture around us, we often take children for granted. We notice them only when they are noisy or get in our way. Frank and Ginny Maier said: "The opposite of love isn't hate; it's indifference." [4] One thing is certain — Jesus was not indifferent to children. But our society is another matter. Look at the way we spend our money. Even the church might learn a lesson from Jesus in this regard. Loving children, Jesus recognized that they were the future leaders of the church and subjects of His kingdom. They were the younger members of the Lord's family. He treated them as intelligent beings and respected their individuality.[5] The sound of their unrestrained voices and spontaneity entranced Him.

Consider what Jesus did for children and how much they meant to Him. He accepted the five loaves and two fish from a small boy and provided for the needs of the multitude by feeding them with the lunch. Jesus healed children. You recall the little boy the disciples could not heal, and the daughter of Jairus whom He raised from the dead. He enjoyed their manner of life, their play, and took note of their games (Matt. 11:16, 17). Our Saviour must have regarded these little ones with a kind of sacred awe. "For I say unto you, That in heaven their angels do always behold the face of my Father which is in heaven" (Matt. 18:10).

Consider the time Jesus cleansed the Temple just before His crucifixion. The priests and rulers came to the Temple and found Him healing the sick, restoring sight to the blind, and making the deaf to hear and the cripples walk. "The children were foremost in the rejoicing. Jesus had healed their maladies; He had clasped them in His arms, received their kisses of grateful affection, and some of them had fallen asleep upon His breast as He was teaching the people. Now with glad voices the children sounded His praise. They repeated the hosannas of the day before, and waved palm branches triumphantly before the Saviour. The temple echoed and reechoed with their acclamations, 'Blessed be he that cometh in the name of the Lord!'"[6]

Indignant, the priests and rulers tried to stop their

demonstrations, but the children kept on shouting and praising Jesus. And what can we learn from this incident? Perhaps we ought to make more room in our worship services for children—their stories, their songs, their praises. We like it when they are quiet and sit with folded hands. But that is not their nature. God "put the wiggles in their legs," and when we fight the wiggles, we oppose Him. Don't misunderstand me. I am not arguing here for irreverence and boisterous behavior. Rather, I am simply saying that the exuberance of children, their spontaneity, their active natures, should be something to encourage rather than to repress—even in Sabbath school or worship service.

Children are naturally drawn to people with a kindly demeanor. Something about Jesus' face attracted the children. His kind, gentle manner won their love, and they followed Him gladly. We repeat again a seminal statement from Ellen White: "In His teaching He came down to their level. He, the Majesty of heaven, did not disdain to answer their questions, and simplify His important lessons to meet their childish understanding."[7] It is our job, as Christian educators, to adapt our curriculum and methods to the child, and not the child to our curriculum and methods. As we have said earlier, it is so vital to know where the learner is in his or her developmental process. It is all too true that we "look upon the world of children as a stranger." We think we remember what it was like to be 4, or 10, or 15 years old, but we really don't. This is why age level grading is so vital. "The Lord had directed that even from babyhood the children should be taught of His goodness and His greatness, especially as revealed in His law, and shown in the history of Israel. Song and prayer and lessons from the Scriptures were to be adapted to the opening mind."[8]

How easy it is for parents and teachers to be deaf to the questions of children. Not so with Jesus. His great love for children caused Him to respect them and listen to them. Mark says that "he took the children in his arms, put his hands on them and blessed them" (Mark 10:16, NIV). Children know that you care for them, not by the words that you speak, but by a hug, a hand on the shoulder, or just a touch. We have spoken before about skin hunger. They need to be touched many times a day. Jesus recognized this fact, and constantly did so. As we have said before, Jesus was a "toucher." He touched the lepers, the blind eyes, the deaf, and the discouraged.

I enjoy teaching children and like to be around them, to play with them. (It helps keep me young.) I like to watch them explore and discover. They wonder what happens to water when you splash it or why sand feels different from water. Let us learn to be close observers of children, to train ourselves to study their behavior.

I am sure that Jesus often got down on the ground to play with children. He must have picked flowers and helped them to discover their beauty. The Master Teacher knew that childhood learning is natural and pleasurable and an inborn instinct. "Some delightful films made by the late Dr. Arnold Gesell of Yale University show little creatures who can barely talk investigating problems with all the zeal and excitement of explorers, making discoveries with the passion and absorption of dedicated scientists. At the end of each successful investigation, there comes over each tiny face an expression of pure heartfelt pleasure."[9]

"What a blessing it would be if all would teach as Jesus taught!"[10]

[1] White, *The Desire of Ages*, p. 184.

[2] ———, *Christ's Object Lessons*, p. 17.

[3] *Ibid.*, p. 21.

[4] Frank and Ginny Maier, "A Second Chance at Life," *Reader's Digest*, Dec. 1991, p. 210.

[5] White, *The Desire of Ages*, p. 515.

[6] *Ibid.*, p. 592.

[7] *Ibid.*, p. 515.

[8] *Ibid.*, p. 69.

[9] Gilbert Highet, "The Pleasures of Learning," *Reader's Digest*, Sept. 1976, p. 95.

[10] White, *Counsels on Sabbath School Work*, p. 182.

Chapter 14

Creative Family Worships

Y̶ou have heard about the Great Depression of
the 1930s, but few of you who read these
words experienced it. I well recall the long
lines in front of the soup kitchens in down-
town Portland, Oregon, and remember seeing hundreds
of desperate men hanging on freight trains on their way
to the next town to look for work. One day my parents
received word that the person holding the mortgage on
our business and home was going to foreclose. Mother
gathered us children into the bedroom. We had an in-
tense session of prayer. The next day she went to visit
the mortgage holder with a request that he accept the
government's offer to guarantee mortgages in order to
save homes (Home Owners' Loan Corporation). It
seemed hopeless, but we claimed God's promise. Later
in the day she returned all smiles and said, "God has
heard our prayers. He accepted the government's plan."
Our home and business were saved.

During those days we learned the meaning of
"wrestling with God in prayer." My faith strengthened
as I saw God answer prayer after prayer. Family worship was a regular event at our home.

The Valuegenesis report tells us that only 44 percent of the children in grades 6 to 8 and 31 percent in
grades 9 to 12 report "frequent family worship."[1] In

the conference in which I live a recent survey indicates that only 26 percent of the families have regular family worship. Will it take another great depression or some national catastrophe to revive prayer and family worship in Seventh-day Adventist homes? I hope not. Let's renew family worship on our own iniatitive.

WHY FAMILY WORSHIP?

Some say that we're living in a different time, and that daily family worship is not practical anymore. One man said, "My wife and I both work full-time. I leave at 6:30 a.m. for work. The children catch the school bus at 7:15, and my wife leaves for her work at 7:30. Almost every night it seems there is something going on: band practice, choir practice, church committee meetings, etc. We tried family worship, but it engendered so much bitterness and stress that we finally gave it up."

Seventh-day Adventist homes will have no family worship unless we first recognize its vital importance and are willing to carve out time for God and family togetherness. "Fathers and mothers, however pressing your business, do not fail to gather your family around God's altar. Ask for the guardianship of holy angels in your home." [2]

Let me suggest a few reasons that I think family worship is important. 1. It helps children learn to pray. They begin to recognize the power of prayer as they see their prayers answered. Family prayer and private prayer then become a part of their life structure. 2. Regular family devotions will build a wall of protection around our children. We live in a world that is seductive, corrupt, and sinful. "The youth in this age must be fitted by the grace of Christ to meet and overcome evils which have been introduced into society. . . . There should be a living, growing interest in storing the mind with Bible truth. The precious knowledge thus gained will build a barrier about the soul."[3] 3. Family worship helps to create family solidarity. Our hectic age makes family togetherness and a genuine closeness hard to achieve. 4. Regular morning and evening family worship will "turn the hearts of the fathers to their children, and the hearts of the children to their fathers" (Mal. 4:6, NIV).

I remember many times when our children were growing up that I found it necessary to apologize: "Son, I'm sorry for losing my temper this morning. I said some things that were very harsh, and I ask for your forgiveness."

"Oh, Dad, it's OK. I forgive you. I know I was a real slowpoke. I'm sorry too." We hugged and felt genuine closeness.

5. Family devotions make God happy. Prayers ascending to Him from sincere Christian families bring Him great joy. "Morning and evening the heavenly universe take notice of every praying household."[4]

Family worships can be "intensely interesting," "enjoyable," and full of life. In order to make this possible, worship should "be short and spirited," "to the point," and "varied."[5]

FAMILY WORSHIP STRATEGIES

1. Plan a series of worships around stories of specific topics such as angels. Look up "angels" in a concordance, and it will give you lots of Bible passages containing interesting stories. 2. Select a Bible story in which the characters dialogue. (The parable of the great banquet, Luke 14:15-24; the story of Lazarus,

John 11:3-44; etc.) Assign family members to read the various parts. A narrator reads the connecting phrases. 3. Find 10 proverbs that you think have meaning for families today and talk about how we can apply them to family life. 4. Choose a Bible story ahead of time and ask the children to act it out. 5. Read a continuous story suitable for the age levels of your children. 6. Discuss sex education for worship as a part of God's beautiful plan for humanity. Adapt it to your children's age levels. 7. Use nature items for spiritual object lessons. 8. Memorize Bible texts or chapters as a family project. 9. Play the game Twenty Questions, using Bible characters. 10. Read a devotional book through together, various family members taking turns reading paragraphs. 11. Plan a series of worships around a psalm such as Psalm 1. Read the first verse and discuss its meaning. On the second day, with each child having a Bible, read in unison the first and second verses. This time explain and amplify the second verse, continuing on the third day in the same manner, and so on to the end of the psalm. 12. Again ahead of time, ask the children to select a favorite verse and tell why they like it. 13. Play a "cap verse" game, going around the family circle. The first letter of the last word in a verse is a clue for the next person to repeat a verse beginning with that letter. 14. Begin telling a familiar Bible story and ask the children to guess who the story is about. 15. Share a story about the origin of a song or hymn and then sing the song. 16. Read the twenty-third psalm with each child taking a turn reading a verse. Ask them to underline important words. 17. Help your children to plan and conduct your worships from time to time. 18. Study the children's Sabbath school lesson with them. Make it relevant and interesting. Involve small children by using finger plays or motion songs.[6]

Avoid long prayers; don't moralize; encourage questions; take time to visit with your children—especially on Friday evenings. Share your personal faith journey. Tell of your struggles and answers to prayer. Listen with your heart as your children share their feelings. The Valuegenesis report points to this as a powerful factor in developing a mature faith.

A young Japanese girl whose friends called her "Cherry Blossom" visited a Christian home at Christmas time. Cherry Blossom thoroughly enjoyed her wonderful holiday season with the Clarkson family. After the festivities it came time for Cherry Blossom to return to her home. Mrs. Clarkson, her hostess, stood in the library with her hand on the shoulder of the little Japanese girl she had learned to love. "Now, tell me before you go, how you like the way we American folks live? Are you weary of sitting on chairs and sleeping in beds and wearing shoes all day long?"

"Oh, I love it!" she said. "Your home is wonderful!" Then her eyes grew suddenly wistful. "But—" she hesitated.

"But what?" asked Mrs. Clarkson.

"There's one thing I miss," the girl replied with a faraway look in her eyes, "that makes your home seem queer to me. You know, I have been with you to your church and I have seen you worship your God there. But I have missed the God in your home. You know, in Japan, we have a god shelf in every house, with the gods right there in our homes. Do Americans worship their God in their homes?"

Mrs. Clarkson thought a long time after her guest

had gone. She decided right then and there to reestablish the family altar.[7]

IT'S TIME TO REPAIR THE ALTAR

Do you remember the story of Elijah and the false prophets on Mount Carmel? When no answer came from Baal, Elijah said to all the people, "Come here to me." He then "repaired the altar of the Lord, which was in ruins. Elijah took twelve stones. . . . With the stones he built an altar in the name of the Lord" (1 Kings 18:30-32, NIV). The prophet prayed. "Then the fire of the Lord fell and burned up the sacrifice. . . . When all the people saw this, they fell prostrate and cried, 'The Lord—he is God! The Lord—he is God!'" (verses 38, 39, NIV). Modern Israel, like ancient Israel, desperately needs revival. Let us pray for the outpouring of the Spirit as Elijah prayed for rain, and the spiritual refreshing will come. What is the condition of your family altar? If it is broken, take the initiative and reestablish it. And if you are currently conducting regular family worship, think how you can improve it. I hope you will consider some of the above suggestions and teach the Bible creatively through family worship.

---

[1] *Valuegenesis Report I*, p. 28.

[2] White, *Child Guidance*, p. 520.

[3] ———, *Counsels on Sabbath School Work*, p. 36.

[4] ———, *Child Guidance*, p. 519.

[5] *Ibid.*, pp. 521, 522.

[6] The preceding suggestions were adapted in part from Harvey and Kathy Corwin, *Rescuing Family Worship*, pp. 3-7.

[7] Adapted from a sermon by J. L. Tucker entitled "Family Altar."

The Moral and Spiritual
Life of Children and Youth

The ultimate disease of our time is valuelessness.
. . . This state is more crucially dangerous than
ever before in history," Abraham H. Maslow, a
foremost spokesman of humanistic psychology,
wrote to my great surprise. He went on to lament the
"rootlessness, emptiness, hopelessness, the lack of something to believe in and to be devoted to." [1] While walking through a bookstore recently, I noticed the large
number of titles on values, ethics, and moral behavior.
An outcry and revolt seems to be rising in America
against criminal activity.

Can we really expect anything else when so many
parents and teachers subscribe to a value-free philosophy? "Everything is relative, you know." And so we
leave our children and youth to drift on a sea of rela-
tivism. How would it affect your behavior if you believed that the here and now is all there is? As someone
said, "What does bad have to do with good in a world of
chance?" Speaking of sin, Karl Menninger said that it
disappeared from our use, but "perhaps it has not gone
from the back of our minds." [2]

The purpose of this chapter is to look more closely at
the moral and spiritual life of our children and youth.

We would like to help our kids "find true north on the compass of their lives." I am profoundly grateful for the Holy Scriptures, a perfect standard of truth: "I will make justice the measuring line and righteousness the plumb line" (Isa. 28:17, NIV). But God does more than give us guidelines. He provides the power to change our hearts and enables us to be obedient to Christ. Moreover, He gives us the desire to reach His ideal.

How can we help our youth find their way through this world of moral confusion and conflict? They make so many of their important decisions on the basis of peer pressure, unthinking acquiescence to authority, or powerful propaganda. Our challenge is to help them develop a process for selecting the best.

THINKING MORALLY

You may have heard of Derrick Proctor's study of 415 seniors at nine Seventh-day Adventist high schools in four Midwestern states. Testing them with some of Kohlberg's moral dilemmas, he made a shocking discovery. He found that our adolescent students "demonstrated a relatively low level of moral maturity when compared with subjects in other studies."[3]

Roger L. Dudley observes that the research does not demonstrate that the behavior of Adventist youth is less moral than other young people. As a matter of fact, he thinks it was undoubtedly better. What we are considering here is not behavior, but rather *reasons* for behavior. Perhaps it's because parents and teachers have focused so strongly on correct behavior based on rules that we have not assisted our youth to internalize the principles and understand the reasons for their behavior.[4] Keeping children in control through rewards and punishment certainly does not advance their reasoning along moral lines. Have we been guilty of brainwashing our children in the name of character so their judgment in these areas lags behind?

What can we do, then, to help our children and youth think clearly about the reasons for their moral behavior? Free and open discussion will enable youth to discover the reasons behind our standards. Dudley says that we should "encourage teenagers to question our value statements. . . . We *must* press adolescents to raise the questions, identify the issues, and think through to the solutions, or they will reach adulthood with a set of 'values' that can easily collapse and disappear in a crisis because they have never been personally committed to them."[5] Yes, "freedom is risky." Dudley quotes Rollo May: "'It requires greater courage to preserve inner freedom than to stand defiantly for outer freedom.'"[6] Conformity without coming to thoughtful moral conclusions is dangerous.[7]

Interaction sharpens moral thinking. Parents and teachers need to constantly discuss with their children the *reasons* for what we hold to be true. Help learners to stretch their reasoning powers. Many believe that a person's amount of significant responsibility and individual experiences greatly influences his or her moral maturity. So actual participation in social roles and interpersonal relationships helps educate one for moral maturity. (It is important to match the level of discussion to the pupil's developmental stage, however.)

MORAL EDUCATION IN THE CLASSROOM
(grades 7-12)

Consider the following suggestions and strategies: 1. Confront learners with moral problems. Use current events, political problems, and church issues as grist for discussion of moral dilemmas. 2. Resist the temptation to do all the talking. Clarify, rephrase, and above all, listen supportively. 3. Allow young people to participate in rule-making. 4. Give learners practice in choosing alternatives in everyday situations. 5. Don't use their mistakes as a spring board for discussing moral issues. 6. Don't overreact to what learners say. 7. Role plays, charades, and sociodramas are especially valuable in helping children to think and to "feel" the problems. 8. Remember, shaming does not teach.

CHILDREN AND CONVERSION

A pastor overheard the director of his preschool division (ages 0 to 6) teaching the children to repeat the Lord's Prayer. "He entered the room and interrupting the superintendent, said: 'You must not teach them to pray "Our Father," for God is not their father; they are of their father the devil.'"[8] Are our unbaptized children lost? Are they children of the devil because they have not experienced conversion? When does a child, growing up in a devout Christian home, become a "Christian"? What is a Christian—a believer in Jesus, a church member, or what? Must a child be regenerated, born again, and baptized before he or she is a Christian?

Robert Coles, professor of psychiatry at Harvard University, tells of a moving experience that happened to him during the desegregation struggle in New Orleans. Ruby Bridges, a 6-year-old Black child, braved the murderous heckling of the mobs to attend the Frantz school. Every day the federal marshals took her to school and brought her home. Every day Ruby faced the shouting, cursing mob. When a woman spat at her, Ruby turned and smiled. Another man shook his fist, and she smiled at him, too. "Then she walked up the stairs, and she stopped and turned and smiled one more time! You know what she told one of the marshals? She told him she prays for those people, the ones in that mob, every night before she goes to sleep!" [9]

Her behavior mystified teachers, counselors, and psychiatrists. How could this 6-year-old girl stand up against such adversity? Coles asked Ruby about her prayers. The child replied tersely, "Yes, I do pray for them . . ." "I was curious about why she would want to pray for people who were being so unswervingly nasty to her. 'I go to church,' she told me, 'every Sunday, and we're told to pray for everyone, even the bad people, and so I do.'" [10]

Coles found her to be a very normal buoyant little girl. He tried to understand her as the weeks turned into months and she braved the heckling crowds every morning. In time Ruby told how the minister had come to their house to encourage her. The pastor explained that if she continued to forgive and smile and pray for them, God would keep an eye on everything and all would work out well.

In looking back over these events, Coles said that his experience with Ruby in New Orleans changed the course of his life. And so he spent some 30 years writing about children, interviewing them, and analyzing them—especially their moral and spiritual life. [11]

He tells the story of Connie—a little Catholic girl who clearly recognized the difference between spiritual life and religious life. In looking back over his friendship with her, he said, "Even now I can feel her words getting to me—and getting at a psychological truth." [12] Coles wrote about Mark, the son of a very sincere Seventh-day Adventist family living near Chattanooga. An athlete, Mark said, "I've been lucky that God has picked me. It's

His smile. . . . When I'm running and I see His smile, I feel my body change—it's like shifting into high gear." Mark spoke about his prayer life. "I said my prayers in the morning, and I asked God, please, to let me do the best I could. I didn't ask Him to make me the winner, no, sir. I used to want to win the races, but my daddy and our minister said it's not the winning, it's the running with God's blessing, that's what counts." [13] Coles discovered hundreds of more examples.

In these stories we discover a clue about the "motors of morality." A spiritual dynamic occurs in the life of children that is beautiful and powerful. And it testifies to the power of Christian culture!

SACRAMENTAL OR CONVERSIONIST THEOLOGY

William L. Hendricks says that "sacramental theology also involves a conversionist principle. However, the conversionist principle in sacramental theology is gradual. Sacramental theology stresses grace, infant baptism as a means of receiving grace, the corporate religious experience, and the rites of church tradition as further means of extending grace." [14] From this viewpoint many sacramentalists believe that a child is alienated from God but his or her "alienation is overcome by infant baptism which places the child in grace." [15] A conversionist, however, believes that the way to become a Christian is by Christian conversion. When the time is right, the child makes a choice and becomes a Christian. Conversionist theology holds that there comes an awareness of alienation from God and a recognition of God's provision of salvation through Christ.

Many parents struggle with the question "When is my child ready for conversion?" Unfortunately, their anxiety and sometimes that of pastors for unconverted children has led them to pressure children for baptism. (It is often a problem of evangelists who are eager to reap all they can and enlarge the number of their baptisms.)

We certainly would not accept the notion that because children have not yet been baptized, they are children of the devil. Concerning the children of believers, Paul says, "They are holy" (1 Cor. 7:14, NIV). "As soon as a child can love and trust his mother, then can he love and trust Jesus as the Friend of his mother. Jesus will be his Friend, loved and honored. . . . The first lesson that children are to be taught is that God is their Father. This lesson should be given them in their earliest years."[16] "The little children may be Christians, having an experience in accordance with their years."[17] Karl Barth insists that "children . . . are in the kingdom . . . but not in the church, and that parents ought to know this!"[18]

Clifford Ingle gives us some helpful guidelines about the conversion of children. I will endeavor to summarize in part his valuable discussion. 1. He said that accountability is more important than the concept of age. "It is highly doubtful that many children below the age of 9 can express or have experienced despair for sin as radical separation from God. One cannot be 'saved' until he is aware he is 'lost.'"[19] 2. We should not set an arbitrary age for conversion. Children simply do not all mature at the same time. 3. Teachers and leaders should spend much time counseling children and talking with them about their religious experience. Young people need nurture in the path of grace. It is true that conversion does come at a point in time, but it is wrong to force that moment by confronting the child with an experience he or she is not ready to have or understand. 4. He stresses the importance of teaching parents an awareness of the covenant mercy God has toward children and of helping parents to put aside their fears.[20]

ELLEN WHITE'S EXPERIENCE OF CONVERSION

Ellen White shares the story of her conversion. During the March 1840 William Miller meetings in Portland, Maine, Ellen Harmon, age 12, responded to a call for sinners to come forward and confess Christ. She apparently failed to initially experience the joy of salvation because "there was in my heart a feeling that I could never become worthy to be called a child of God." She tells about spending "the long hours of darkness in prayer and tears" and a hesitation to share her feelings with her friends or even her parents. The next summer she attended a Methodist camp meeting in Buxton, Maine. "I was fully resolved to seek the Lord in earnest there, and obtain, if possible, the pardon of my sins." The speaker counseled those who were wavering and fearful to surrender themselves to God and accept His mercy. "All that was required of the sinner, trembling in the presence of his Lord, was to put forth the hand of faith and touch the scepter of His grace. . . . I now began to see my way more clearly, and the darkness began to pass away. I earnestly sought the pardon of my sins, and strove to give myself entirely to the Lord. . . . Suddenly my burden left me, and my heart was light." [21]

Donald M. Joy told of an experience in the early days of his ministry as a youth pastor. He said that he had been observing Mark and had noticed a change taking place in him. Sensing that the boy was reaching out after the Lord, Joy watched for an opportunity to talk to him. The opportunity came one Saturday night after a church social. Joy offered to take the boy home. They pulled up in front of Mark's house and started to talk. After discussing some trivial things, the pastor came to the point: "Mark, have you ever thought of giving your heart to Christ and being baptized?"

After a long pause, the youngster finally said, "Yes, I have thought a lot about it lately. But I don't know how to go about it."

"Would you like me to share the steps with you?"

"Yes, I would appreciate that."

So Joy outlined the simple steps in becoming a Christian. "Mark, would you like to make the surrender tonight?" Another long pause. Finally the boy squirmed in his seat and said, "Yes, I would." Joy prayed and then Mark prayed. He confessed his sins and accepted Jesus Christ as Lord and Saviour.

Here is an example of an alert Bible teacher. He picked up the signals and decided that the time was right. It reminds me of Ellen White's words: "There should be zealous, faithful workers in our Sabbath schools, who will watch and discern upon whom the Spirit of God is moving, and cooperate with the angels of God in winning souls to Christ."[22]

And that's the message I have tried to share with you in this chapter and in this book. Teaching the Bible creatively and with power means helping our children, youth, and adults to think morally and to choose wisely. It requires providing an atmosphere for spiritual and intellectual growth. And it means watching for the signs of the working of God's Spirit and then cooperating with Christ in enabling our children and youth to cross over the threshold into God's glorious kingdom.

[1] Abraham H. Maslow, *Religions, Values, and Peak Experiences* (New York: Penguin Books, 1970), p. 82.

[2] Karl Menninger, *Whatever Became of Sin?* (Toronto: Bantam Books, 1978), p. 28.

[3] Roger L. Dudley, *Passing On the Torch* (Hagerstown, Md.: Review and Herald Pub. Assn., 1986), p. 95.

[4] *Ibid.*, pp. 95-98.

[5] *Ibid.*, p. 66.

[6] *Ibid.*

[7] See White, *Education*, p. 230.

[8] Clifford Ingle, *Children and Conversion* (Nashville: Broadman Press, 1970), p. 11.

[9] Robert Coles, *The Moral Life of Children* (New York: Grove/Atlantic, Inc., 1986), p. 23.

[10] *Ibid.*, p. 23.

[11] See Robert Coles, *The Spiritual Life of Children* (Boston: Houghton-Mifflin Com., 1990), pp. xi, xvi.

[12] *Ibid.*, p. 16.

[13] *Ibid.*, p. 49.

[14] William L. Hendricks, *A Theology for Children* (Nashville: Broadman Press, 1980), p. 15.

[15] *Ibid.*, p. 15.

[16] White, *Child Guidance*, pp. 486, 487.

[17] ———, *The Desire of Ages*, p. 515.

[18] Ingle, p. 12.

[19] *Ibid.*, p. 95.

[20] *Ibid.*, pp. 95, 96.

[21] Ellen G. White, *Testimonies*, vol. 1, pp. 14-17.

[22] ———, *Counsels on Sabbath School Work*, p. 11.

Author Index